Donated by

Vera Bankovich

In Honor of the 50th
Wedding Anniversary of

Mr. and Mrs.
Robert L. Cotter, Sr.

NICE SHOT,
MR. NICKLAUS

NICE SHOT, MR. NICKLAUS

STORIES ABOUT THE GAME OF GOLF

MICHAEL KONIK

HUNTINGTON PRESS • LAS VEGAS, NEVADA

Nice Shot, Mr. Nicklaus
Stories About the Game of Golf

Published by
  Huntington Press
  3687 South Procyon Avenue
  Las Vegas, Nevada 89103
  (702) 252-0655 Phone
  (702) 252-0675 Fax
  e-mail: books@huntingtonpress.com

ISBN 0-929712-03-X

Cover Photo: Ginny Dixon
Author Photo: Sandrine Pecher
Cover Design: Laurie Shaw
Interior Design: Bethany Coffey Rihel & Laurie Shaw
Production: Laurie Shaw

"The Canterbury (Golf) Tales" originally appeared in *Golf &
Travel;* "Hacker's Heaven" originally appeared in *Forbes FYI;* all
other stories originally appeared in *SKY*

Printing History
1st Edition—November 2000

To Duncan Christy, my patron and my friend.
Thank you for knowing.

ACKNOWLEDGEMENTS

Deke Castleman is the most sympathetic editor a writer could have, and I am grateful he wields a corrective pencil as expertly as Phil Mickelson does a lob wedge. Lynne Loomis' assiduous copy editing and Bethany Coffey's clever production skills are worthy of a major championship. And Anthony Curtis' clear-headed captaincy would serve America well in a Ryder Cup.

Along with Len, Laurie, and the rest of the able Huntington Press team, the editorial staff of *Sky* magazine is largely responsible for the content of this book, particularly Mickey McLean, who consistently keeps his longtime "Tee Time" columnist in the literary fairway.

Thanks, also, to Neal Bascomb, for seeing this book through from tee to green.

My stories would not be possible if not for the efforts of innumerable people in the golf industry, including professional players, their managers and agents, public-relations operatives, and the countless unseen souls who make a golf course live. Thank you all for being part of a great game.

CONTENTS

PREFACE

Golf is more than a sport, and far more than a pastime. It's a journey and an examination, a diversion and a trial, a romantic love affair and a heart-wrenching betrayal. It's a tidy little metaphor for being alive, rich in symbolism and even richer in sentiment. That's why I love writing about it.

More than five years ago, an editor colleague contacted me with an intriguing assignment. He'd been hired to overhaul *Sky*, the in-flight publication of Delta Air Lines. Somehow—demographic research? intuition?—this visionary editor got the idea that his millions of readers, weary from missed connections and time-zone changes, would find some joy in reading about the game of golf. Every issue.

"I'm thinking about having a regular golf column in the magazine," he explained. "I mean, every month. I know the average road warrior is going to love reading about top players and great courses. And I'd like them to look forward to our golf coverage every time they pick up a new issue."

Sounds great, I told him.

"I'm just concerned about one thing," he confessed. "Do you think it's possible to come up with twelve interesting stories a year, month after month?"

What was "in play," I wondered?

"Everything. Travel. Profiles. Human interest. Equipment. Competitions. Everything."

Give me a day or two, I told him.

The next morning I faxed him a list of three dozen story ideas.

"I think we may have something here," he said.

Indeed, we still do. The game of golf is like a magical well that never runs dry, even in the hottest months. There are always fascinating people to meet, faraway courses to visit, powerful lessons to learn. This collection of stories features some of my favorites. You'll find countless other tales in your weekend foursome, on a remote tee overlooking the sea, in your heart.

Golf gives and gives. I'm honored to share some of its treasures.

Michael Konik
August 15, 2000
Los Angeles

1

Nice Shot, Mr. Nicklaus

"Are you sure?" he asks, regarding me with an unwavering gaze, like a high-stakes poker player searching for a faint pulse of apprehension in his opponent's neck.

"Yes, sir," I say, with as much conviction as I can muster, given the circumstances. The truth is, I *was* sure about 10 seconds ago. I was certain. I'd looked at the putt from both sides of the hole. I'd noted the direction water was meant to drain off the green. And, when he asked me, I told my man, "It moves right to left, just a bit."

I had no doubt.

But now he's plumb-bobbing the putt, one eye squinted shut, frowning slightly. He looks like he ate something sour. "Right to left?" he asks, incredulous. "You're sure? You're completely positive?" He plumb-bobs the putt once more. "I don't know, Mike. It looks like it could be left to right."

This isn't the 18th at Augusta National; the Ryder Cup is not on the line. But considering my heart rate at the moment, it might as well be. I am standing on the 2nd green at Grand Haven Golf Club in Palm Coast, Florida, staring down a putt that means absolutely nothing in the grand scheme of competitive golf—not even a $5 bet is at stake, let alone the Open Championship—yet never before have I so wanted to read a green correctly.

I look my man in the eyes, the same eyes that have seen more drama and history upon a golf course than any eyes in the world, and I say firmly, "I believe the putt moves right to left, sir."

"You're positive," he says again, flatly.

Well, no. Actually, I am most definitely not positive. Because one does not disagree about the line of a putt with the greatest golfer of all time. I consider saying something like, "You're the boss" or, more to the point, "Why are you asking *me* for advice? *You're* the one who designed the damned green." But instead, at the risk of losing whatever shred of esteem I may have earned from the master, I nod my head affirmatively.

"Yes, sir," I lie. "I'm absolutely sure it's right to left."

"Good!" Jack Nicklaus says, smiling mischievously, like a duffer whose drive bounces off an out-of-bounds stake into the middle of the fairway. "I just wanted to make sure you weren't a yes man." He winks at me and addresses his ball, aiming just off the edge of the cup, to allow for the putt's right-to-left break.

I'll never win the Open. But at least I know what it must feel like.

❖ ❖ ❖

Other sports have numerous candidates for Best Ever, Finest This, and Most Outstanding That. Fans with apparently not much else to do fill the radio airwaves with impassioned and compelling cases for a legion of worthy heroes: Louis, Marciano, and Ali in boxing; Chamberlain, Abdul-Jabbar, and Jordan in basketball; Cobb, Ruth, and Mays in baseball.

Golf does not invite such a discussion. Jack Nicklaus' record as a player of championship tournament golf is, and probably always will be, unequaled. He is the greatest. Ever. And until Tiger Woods (or anyone else for that matter) surpasses Jack's career totals in major victories, that's all there is to say on that matter.

Funny, though: A hundred years from now, when anyone who ever saw the man play golf will be long dead, when the living will never have known his ferocious power (or his equally ferocious determination), the name Jack Nicklaus will still be uttered with a reverential whisper. But it won't be because of the number of times he won major championships.

It will be because of the golf courses he left behind.

As he enters the twilight of his life—a life, it should be noted, that has been blessed on and off the links—Jack Nicklaus has become a part-time player and a full-time architect. He competes in a few important tournaments each year—when you're 60 and still a threat to win the Masters, there's an unwritten rule (which I hereby decree) that says you are *required* to make a go of it—and intends to continue doing so until the year 2000, when, he claims, he will more or less say farewell to competitive golf. But the bulk of his working life these days is dedicated to designing some of the most memorable golf courses on the planet. Like the trees that surround them and the rivers that run through them, these golf courses will remain for many years where Jack left them, serving as verdant playgrounds for millions of aspiring hackers. Clubs in hand, these duffers will retrace Jack's steps along the tracks he laid out many decades previous. And they'll dream, as we all do, of one day playing as wondrously as this legendary Nicklaus fellow they've read about in the record books.

Jack Nicklaus has his name on 164 courses, including 138 solo designs, open for play around the world. His architectural vision, expressed in dirt and grass, water and sand, may presently be found in 26 countries and 29 states. That figure is sure to grow before the Golden Bear goes into permanent hibernation: Fifty-six other Nicklaus Design courses are now under construction or are being conceived. Canny developers, who know a Jack Nicklaus golf course sells real estate and fills resorts and attracts professional tournaments more effectively than any other, are fairly tripping over themselves to pay $1 million or more for Jack's next creation.

I've played Jack Nicklaus golf courses in six countries. Some I have liked, some I have disliked. Some I hated, some I loved. All of them, though, had one quality in common: They were built carefully and beautifully, with no expense spared in the pursuit of aesthetic pleasure and shot-making fun.

Twice in 1998 I attended gala opening celebrations, where Jack Nicklaus inaugurated one of his new golf courses with an exhibition round. On both occasions, at Laurel Springs near Atlanta and Reflection Bay in Las Vegas, Jack, employing a clip-on microphone, explained to the gallery following him why he made each hole as he had—why a bunker here, why a dogleg there, why the green was sloped in one direction, why the fairway flowed in another. It's been said that no one has ever *thought* himself around a golf course as well as Jack Nicklaus. Hearing the man explain his design ethos as he played, I was inclined to agree.

Still, I wanted to sit down with him, face to face, and ask him a few questions about designing golf courses. The straight dope. Getting a few minutes of Jack Nicklaus' undivided attention, however, would be the same as being granted an audience with the Pope—only it's twice as difficult. So when I learned I could have 10 or 15 minutes with him at Grand Haven, his last course-opening event of the year, I was delighted. Little did I know my 10 minutes would turn into six hours.

❖ ❖ ❖

This is the kind of thought you have when you meet Jack Nicklaus as he arrives at the front door of Grand Haven Golf Club: "Wow. That man right there, the one with sandy blonde hair, the one who looks exactly like Jack Nicklaus—that's Jack Nicklaus!" In other words, there's something stupefying and impossible about standing on a gravel driveway, unloading golf clubs from the back of a sport utility vehicle, while the greatest golfer of all time stands nearby, chatting amiably with awestruck dignitaries who must exercise every ounce of discipline in their multimillionaire bodies not to ask him for an autograph.

What's even stranger is to be left alone in a locker room with the greatest golfer of all time as he stretches, puts in his contact lenses, and changes into his playing attire. Not in my most hallucinatory dreams did I ever imagine I might see Jack Nicklaus in his underwear.

Of course, I never imagined I would be serving as his caddie, either. But shortly after I came to Grand Haven, Jack's public relations people said they had a little surprise for me. In the journalism business, this usually means your scheduled interview has been canceled. Instead, they needed someone to carry Jack's bag.

Would I be interested? That was like asking if I might volunteer to be Nicole Kidman's personal hair brusher.

After some intensive and exhaustive research—playing the golf course myself—I was given a special yardage book by one of Grand Haven's helpful assistant professionals. It contained all the information I would need to give my man an accurate "number," as caddies say.

All I had to do was add and subtract.

And keep the clubs clean. And tend the flag. And rake bunkers. And replace divots. And wash golf balls. And stand in the right place. And carry a 150-pound side of beef on my back. And not stutter too badly when I addressed the greatest golfer of all time.

Easy.

❖ ❖ ❖

When caddying for Jack Nicklaus, your mantra is: "Show up, keep up, and above all, shut up." I was made to understand this by Scott Tolley, Jack's director of communications. (Having achieved a certain station in life, men like Mr. Nicklaus have private pilots, personal ghostwriters, and directors of various pursuits.) Knowing I had some previous experience caddying for my boyhood neighbor Skip Kendall, a rising star on the PGA Tour, Tolley was confident I'd do a reasonable job of lugging around his boss' clubs. Still, he was required to make The Speech, which all of Jack's honorary caddies get before slinging the fancifully decorated staff bag over their shoulders.

Jack, Tolley tells me, has a couple of idiosyncrasies involving the freshness of golf balls and the descriptions of yardage distances, which I will promptly come to know and appreciate and not question. Jack, he tells me, does not need, desire, or tolerate advice on how to play a golf hole, especially when it's one he has designed. And Jack, he tells me with quiet emphasis, *hates* to be "clubbed." That is to say, under no circumstances whatsoever am I to recommend a specific club ("I think a smooth 7-iron should do, big guy!") to my man.

I laugh when I hear this rule. As if I, a mere golf writer, would dare to tell Jack Nicklaus—*Jack Nicklaus!*—what club he ought to hit! Does a member of his church choir tell Jose Carreras how much vibrato to use in *Carmen*? Does the school lunch lady suggest to Alain Ducasse how much pepper he should use in his *coq au vin*? You don't instruct the master. You hope to absorb a few milligrams of his greatness, perhaps through osmosis, if not more conventional means.

❖ ❖ ❖

My loop with the Golden Bear begins awkwardly. I'm nervous as a cat in a dog pound. After stroking three quick putts on the practice green, Jack asks me, "Are the greens out on the course about this fast?" I tell him I honestly don't know. "Well," he says with a trace of irritableness in his voice, "does the grass look the same?" I tell him yes, it does. He shrugs. "Okay. Good enough."

We proceed to Grand Haven's first tee, which is already surrounded by hundreds of astonished onlookers, craning to get a peek at Jack Nicklaus hitting a golf ball. I take my position to the right of the tee box, yardage book in one hand, unsheathed driver in the other. When Mr. Nicklaus approaches me, I hand him the club and he extends his right hand toward me. Instinctively, I shake it.

Quietly, so as not to humiliate me, Jack Nicklaus leans toward me and says, "Uh, Mike? I need you to give me a ball."

"Oh," I say sheepishly, releasing my grip on his hand. "Right. Sorry." I fish a Maxfli Revolution 100 (with JACK printed on it) out of my bib and place it in his palm, feeling as though I am quite possibly the least suave fellow ever to walk the Earth.

After taking a quick glance at my yardage book, Nicklaus explains to the congregation that this hole is a straightforward 406-yard par-4, with bunkers framing the fairway. "Nice little hole," he says, addressing his ball. As Jack Nicklaus goes through his pre-shot routine, taking the familiar waggles I've watched on television all my life, I am gripped with a sudden bout of first-tee terror—and I'm not the one hitting the shot.

For the next four hours or so, Jack Nicklaus is *my* player, my man. I must take care of him. I must help him avoid trouble and find salvation. I must be his guardian. And though this gentleman standing beside me probably feels nothing but pleasure—the pleasure born of serene confidence—I'm scared for him. I want so badly for him to enjoy himself, to feel the satisfying pop of the clubhead meeting the ball, to watch it sail away like a jet-powered pill. I want so badly for Jack Nicklaus, my man, to do well.

I hold my breath. He pulls the club back, sets it at the top well short of parallel, and unleashes an efficient whip, a snap of controlled fury. I'm watching all this from the kind of intimate perspective normally reserved for swing coaches and lovers, and I am thinking, "I know that swing. It's the pure expression of Jack Nicklaus." And that's when I know: Everything will be all right.

Jack Nicklaus turned 60 this year. But he still hits the ball a mile and it still goes wherever he wants it. He may consider himself a shadow of what he once was; he may joke about being an old man playing on one good leg. But based on extremely close observation—like, right next to the guy—Jack Nicklaus, I can testify, still plays the game of golf in a way with which most of us are not, and will never be, familiar.

Shuffling as fast as I can with Jack's bag bouncing off my hip, I arrive at his ball, safely in the fairway, well before he does. While he signs autographs, I have time to double- and triple-check my yardage, both to the front of the green and to the pin. When he arrives, I am well-prepared, if slightly winded.

"Whadda we got?" Jack Nicklaus says to me.

"One sixty-two to the front of the green. One sixty-nine to the pin," I say, as matter-of-factly as my palpitating heart will allow.

Jack nods. I tip the bag toward him and he extracts a 6-iron. For a moment I consider saying something caddie-like, something quasi-supportive, such as "good tempo" or "focus." Instead, I stand back and pray this shot doesn't end up beyond the green or 30 yards short of it. Because then I would have to flee.

Nicklaus makes perfect contact and sends the ball in a graceful parabola right at the pin. As it's in the air, he says, "That's as good as I can hit it."

And then the ball lands in the front bunker.

As the gallery groans, he looks at me. "One sixty-two?"

"Yes, sir," I say, feeling as though the audience of property owners and invited guests might be on the verge of turning into a nicely dressed and deeply tanned lynch mob.

"Hmmm," Jack says, perplexed. "Good as I can hit it."

I want to say, "Have you considered that the shot was playing slightly uphill and the wind was blowing directly against you?" But I know enough to show up, keep up, and shut up—hoping I'm not in really big trouble.

As I trudge up the fairway, checking my yardage book once more, frightened that suddenly I may be losing my capacity to add seven to 155, one of Jack's many handlers trots up beside me. "Don't worry," he says, waving his own yardage book. "I checked. That yardage was right on."

Four holes later, after my second-green character test,

after several dead-on yardage calls, after a near-eagle and a tap-in birdie, Jack Nicklaus turns to me as we prepare for his second shot on the sixth, "a pretty little par-four," in his words. He said, "You're taking this pretty seriously, aren't you, Mike?"

"Yes, sir, I am."

"No prize money, nothing at stake," Nicklaus says, chuckling, reaching for a pitching wedge. "You're working pretty hard."

"Well, I hear you're a good tipper," I say.

Jack Nicklaus smiles at me and proceeds to stick his approach shot within six-feet. "Shot, pro," I say as Nicklaus hands me the club.

"Thanks," he says, still chuckling.

Jack hits many fine shots this day at Grand Haven, and there are times that I want to look Mr. Nicklaus in the eye and quote the young Scottish caddie who worked for Bobby Jones at St. Andrews. I want to say, "My, but you're a wonder, sir."

Instead, when Jack does something really nice—crush a driver off the fairway to nearly reach a 575-yard par-5 in two; spit a low-running 1-iron into and under a howling wind; boom a towering, Nicklausesque 3-iron over all the trouble in front of a heavily bunkered green and make the ball land like a butterfly with sore feet—when he does what we have all come to expect and desire of Jack Nicklaus, I say to him softly, "Golf shot."

And he knows what I'm trying to say.

❖ ❖ ❖

We're on the 14th hole, a lovely par-three with a green set into a grove of tropical trees. My man has exactly 175 yards to the pin, which sits in front of a steep ridge. I've watched him now for 13 holes. I know what he can do. And I've gotten familiar enough with him to speak up when there's a bit of wind or when a shot plays slightly uphill or when there's a particularly nasty section of green. And I know now that, today, on the 14th hole at Grand Haven, Jack Nicklaus must play a 5-iron.

"Whadda we got?" my man asks.

"One-sixty to the front, one-seven-five to the hole, with a ridge behind." I tip the bag toward Jack Nicklaus—with his 5-iron sticking halfway out.

"So now you're a mind reader," he says, grabbing the club.

"That's the stick, sir," I say, violating the one inviolable rule of caddying for Jack Nicklaus.

He takes a practice swing. "Mike, what kind of golfer are you?"

"I'm an 8-handicap, sir."

"And what kind of writer are you?"

"As a writer, sir, I'd like to think I'm a little better than scratch."

Jack Nicklaus laughs heartily—and lands his tee shot 10 feet from the flag, pin high.

"Shot," I say, grinning. "Of course, it may have been the club."

"I believe you're right," Jack Nicklaus says.

For the remainder of the round, we joke back and forth. Nicklaus has a refined seldom appreciated sense of humor. On one hole he offers to let me putt for him, since he hasn't made a birdie in six tries. (I decline, lest I soil myself.) On another hole, he asks me what I think the chances of him chipping in from off the fringe might be. I tell him 20 percent, one out of five.

He misses the chip. "Give me another ball," Jack says. He tries again and misses.

"One more," he says, Tin Cup-like. He tries again and makes it.

"I think it's more like thirty-three percent," Jack says.

❖ ❖ ❖

We're standing together on the 18th green. Jack has just blasted a sand shot to within a foot for an easy par. I'm holding his putter, waiting to hand it to him, and I realize I'm holding the putter that made a run at the '98 Masters, the putter he'll probably be using this year at the U.S. Open. Jack Nicklaus' putter.

It feels like any other putter, but there's magic about it.

Likewise, the golf ball I take home with me from Grand Haven feels like any other golf ball. But there's magic about it, too. The ball has the date of Grand Haven's opening written on it, and it says, "Thanks, Mike. Jack Nicklaus."

I don't collect memorabilia. But like a lovely golf course that flourishes over the centuries, welcoming visitors of each succeeding generation, the memories this golf ball triggers will remain with me long after I am able to play the game.

HACKERS
AND
THEIR
DREAMS

2

THE COW
PASTURE OPEN

Wisdom, Montana, population 120, has a motel, a gas
station, a post office, a restaurant, a general store, and, this
being the wild frontier, two saloons. And while there's an
art gallery trafficking in Western-type things, forget about
symphony orchestras or opera companies or ballet troupes,
not to mention a movie theater or video store or municipal
swimming pool. There's not even a school.

Wisdom, to be honest, is a five-second visual respite
from Montana highway emptiness.

Which is why Wisdom, Montana, might be among the
least likely candidates in the United States to host a golf
tournament.

Another compelling reason: Wisdom, Montana, doesn't
even have a golf course.

Now, having a golf course might seem like a fairly important, perhaps *utterly necessary*, first step in putting on a
golf tournament. But we're talking about cowboy types here,
not easily dismayed suburbanites. Lacking a golf course did
not strike the rugged folks of Wisdom as much of a reason
not to put on a golf tournament. They figured they would
use what they did have, which is plenty of wide-open, treeless, links-style, cattle land. (The region in which Wisdom
is situated, the Big Hole Valley, is known as "The Land of

10,000 Haystacks," something that cannot be said about, for instance, Augusta, Georgia.) This is the kind of raw untamed land that, were it in the Scottish Highlands, would inspire volumes of impassioned prose in all the golf journals and mandatory pilgrimages from well-financed members of our better country clubs.

But this is Wisdom, Montana, 76 miles from Butte and 121 miles from Missoula. Close to an hour from a proper golf course. Worlds away in spirit from synthetic driving-range mats and custom-fitted irons and heavily promoted graphite shafts.

Still, the people of Wisdom wanted to have a golf tournament. Just because it seemed like an amusing thing to do. Play golf, drink beer, have some laughs. Nothin' serious. They figured a golf tournament might turn into a bona fide *event* and help tourism in the area—if you can call a once-a-year deluge of a hundred or so out-of-towners "tourism." They figured it might put Wisdom on the map, at least for a day or two. But mostly they figured hosting a golf tournament in Wisdom, Montana, just might be a lot of fun.

Fun. Remember that concept? Whether because it's inherently impossible or because its participants tend toward masochism, golf, it seems, seldom breeds fun. Momentary joy, yes; a pleasant day in the park, certainly. But *fun*? No, if you want fun, you play golf of the miniature variety, where getting your ball into the dinosaur's mouth wins a free game. The grown-up version of golf is the stuff of set jaws and steely scowls, of hot sighs and shaking heads.

Not in Wisdom, it's not.

Every year around Labor Day, local rancher Monte Clemow, who owns a little old parcel of land—about 20,000 acres or so—goes out into one of his fields with a shovel. He digs up some holes and puts flags next to them. He puts directional stakes in the ground and big black feed buckets in some spots and sawdust in other places. Then he lets 1,200 or so head of cattle chew the rough grass down to almost playable levels. And that's it. For a few days Monte and his neighbors have a 12-hole golf course. Two of them, actually: Monte usually makes 24 holes and divides them in half. Then Monte and his Wisdom neighbors invite everyone they know to come to town and play golf for the day.

The event is known as the Cow Pasture Open. Participants often wear funny costumes, similar to what you might see at a masquerade ball, with a large contingent opting for the Lone Ranger look. They ride horses and motorcycles or drive trucks and four-wheel all-terrain scooters on the golf course. They drink lots of free beer. They take six hours to play 12 holes. No one cares about scores. Nine or ten is a typical tally on a typical 200-yard hole. There's a *shortest* drive contest. Balls roll into badger holes. Balls roll into cow pies. Balls disappear. There are no greens. There are no yardage markers. There are no rules.

Everyone has fun.

❖ ❖ ❖

The night before the fourth Annual Cow Pasture Open, in 1997, I'm sitting at the bar in Antler's, one of Wisdom's two drinking establishments. This is the kind of place where the jukebox has nothing but country music, and if you don't like Garth Brooks, you'd better keep it to yourself. Parents bring their young children, who fall asleep on the floor next to the pool table while the adults slam back beer and whiskey and, if they're feeling exotic, drinks with fruit juice in 'em. Antler's is buzzing, like the pubs in St. Andrews the night before the Open Championship. "I'm gonna do good," one cowboy promises his drinking mate. "I've played twice this year."

I ask the cowboy if most people prepare for the Cow Pasture Open. "Hell, no," he says, laughing. "Most of us play golf once a year if we're lucky. You play much?" he asks me. I tell him I do. "Oh well then, you'll win," he says.

❖ ❖ ❖

The cowboy, I'm sad to say, is mistaken. I do not play well enough to win. But I have an excuse, of course: I feel way too self-conscious. When I see most of the Cow Pasture Open contestants dressed in their best cowboy duds and wielding persimmon clubs circa 1964, I feel woefully out of place, like a black Jewish homosexual Democrat might feel on the first tee at the Los Angeles Country Club. For a moment I cannot decide which is more embarrassing: my toga-like Egyptian sheik costume that I've brought from home in hopes of winning "best costume" or the fact that I am using an oversized titanium driver.

When I make a brief pre-round survey of Monte Clemow's cow pasture, the cows, who have been shooed off the course, are wandering near the parking area, mooing irritably. I'm not sure if this is because so many club-toting strangers are in their midst or because someone has already fired up a big hickory-smoke barbecue. Cows, in fact, are a recurring theme here. After paying my $20 entry fee, I receive a commemorative Cow Pasture Open bag tag. It's made out of an ear tag, the kind ranchers use to identify their herds. Lunch is roast beef. And the high scorer gets a (man-made) cow-chip trophy.

Following a ceremonial cannon blast, play begins. Even after playing three or four holes, it's difficult, if not impossible, to discern the course's design concept. "Oversized putt-putt" might be the best way to describe the Cow Pasture's architectural quirks, though that might be investing too much credence in the whole scheme. "Goofy" is, perhaps, more accurate. Some holes, like the one that has a plastic feed bucket partially submerged in a dry creek bed, are best played with clever bank shots off rocks. Others require more than an inventive imagination; you need luck. Like the one with a toilet seat over the hole: You can't quite putt over the rim, and most chips bounce out. I take a 13 on that hole.

The course is a 3,000-yard unplayable lie. The cow pasture looks a little like what Royal Troon might look like if the superintendent there had lost his lawn mower. Finding your ball is almost as difficult as getting it in the hole. As far as I could discern, Cow Pasture Open participants do not assess themselves a stroke-and-distance penalty for a lost ball. They just drop another one and have a beer.

Often I find myself "greenside" in two. Most of the holes are between 200 and 300 yards, and I usually hit driver-sand wedge to within 10 or 20 feet. And then it normally takes me four or five additional strokes to hole out. (Imagine a "green" constructed from hardpan and three-inch rough and you'll understand.) Never again will I complain about spiked-up putting surfaces.

Despite the trying playing conditions, the Cow Pasture Open is suffused with good cheer, enthusiastic hollering, and drunken howling. Nobody throws clubs. Nobody whines. Nobody stands, hands on hips, looking toward the sky with thinly veiled disdain. About the only complaining you'll hear at the Cow Pasture Open is when a well-struck ball is sent skidding wayward by an unfortunately positioned cow chip (*"Damn, cow chip got that one!"*), the prevalence of which makes wearing traditional golf shoes highly impractical. Players also complain when the guy driving the beer truck stays away too long.

Generally, though, the Cow Pasture Open is a persuasive reminder that golf is not about perfect swings and impeccable fairways. It's about being outdoors with friends, walking—or, what the heck, driving your pickup truck—through a fertile field, with the Big Sky above you and the land beneath your feet, just as Scottish shepherds did centuries ago. It's about feeling the wind on your back and the sun on your cheeks. It's about failing repeatedly and not letting it bother you.

And it's about occasionally doing exactly what you set out to do, feeling the sweet contact of club-face on ball, sending it high and straight and long, watching it escape the mundane bonds of gravity and soar where you want it to soar, lifting your spirit as the ball zooms toward its final resting place: a big, black, plastic, feed bucket.

That, my friends, is Wisdom.

3

ANSWER: 62,000 STROKES

Among the noble things that sports are supposed to do—build character, teach discipline, and all that—sports are supposed to distill the confusion and chaos of being alive into one definable inarguable truth. Sports are supposed to answer one elemental question: Who wins?

The "why" part of this question—why does one athlete win and another lose?—is usually left to windbags like me to explain. Of the "who," there is no debate. The winner is the person who goes higher, faster, farther, and sometimes lower. Sports are generally the great egalitarians. Anyone is eligible to be that faster-higher-farther person. The evil "isms"—nepotism, racism, jingoism—float about the penumbra of sports, but they ultimately cannot defeat the great athlete. The best *will* win.

Of all the sports one might pursue, golf is perhaps the most telling in its judgment. Unlike in figure skating, gymnastics, and boxing, which often erupt into embarrassing quasi-political power struggles among the judges, finding a winner in golf does not require its competitors to submit to the whims of outside agents. It does not award points for artistic impression. You win a golf tournament by shooting a lower score than everyone else. Period. A golf course has no favorites, no prejudices—only willing victims. Golf is you and your ball, you and your talent, you and your will.

Thus, a golf tournament tells us more explicitly than almost any other athletic contest who is the best.

Which is why a competition like the DuPont World Amateur Handicap Championship may be the most maddening sporting event anyone has ever concocted. It is here, every summer in Myrtle Beach, that someone inevitably plays consistently bad golf—very bad golf, 20-over-par golf—and ends up triumphing over 3,900 other competitors.

A few years ago, it was a fellow named Jerry Berghauser of Richmond, Texas, who earned the crown, thanks to a sterling final-round 94. Jerry's a 24-'capper, which, historically, bodes well. Only once has a scratch or near-scratch player won the World Ammy.

Indeed, the average male participant at this, the world's largest amateur handicap tournament, has a 14.25 handicap. The average woman's is 23.2. The average age of the players is 50.6 years old. Every state in the union is represented, as well as 24 foreign countries. The World Ammy—brought to you by the company behind Surlyn, the stuff of far-flying golf balls—is truly an international congregation, albeit one filled with sandbaggers.

Yes, sandbaggers: those no-good, rotten, scandalous degenerates who managed to post better scores than I did.

❖ ❖ ❖

I play in the #5 flight (there are 43 of them), for players with an 8.4 to an 8.9 handicap. This is the only tournament I know of where a 9 handicap puts you in one of the elite brackets. After 72 holes of *net*—very key word—stroke play, the winners of each flight (containing about 100 players per group) advance to an 18-hole playoff, where, inevitably, a 19 handicap waxes the 4s and 5s.

Any wonder why this is probably the most popular golf tournament on Earth?

At my flight's first round at Tidewater, one of the better—and tougher—golf courses in Myrtle Beach, I'm teamed up with a cross section of the World Ammy field. There's Larry from New York, a guy who takes notes after every hole, tracking his "stats" with frightening thoroughness. Larry shoots a 95 the first day and has plenty to write about. There's Jack, who owns a body shop in Jersey and a condo in Myrtle Beach, and who, after four holes of errant tee shots, threatens to throw his driver into the nearest pond. Which wouldn't be so terrible, considering the guy hits his 3-wood farther than I do my titanium #1. And there's Jeff from Delaware, who won his flight two years ago and advanced to the heavily attended finals at the Dunes Club. He's a 28-year-old ace, who hits it long and straight and typically shoots in the low 80s. Which, in this crowd, will get you some hardware.

And there's me. Me, who opens his assault on the World Ammy title with a depressing 47 on Tidewater's scenic front side. Me, who plays as though he has a prosthetic arm and an old war wound that causes momentary loss of muscle control. My playing partners, I can tell, are wondering: "How did this schmo get stuck in our flight? The guy's got to be at least a fifteen-handicap." Fortunately, I manage a back-nine 40 and am not asked to leave the tournament.

Playing wretchedly in the World Ammy is not, in fact, the worst thing you can do. The worst thing you can do is play too well. Golfers with an 8 or a 9 handicap are not supposed to shoot gross 72s. Carding a net 61—or, for that matter, a 59, as some contestants do every year—doesn't look good. You do not post net 59s at the World Ammy without feeling the wrath of 3,900 other hackers, without having your manhood, honor, and Love of the Game called into question. Frequently overheard are comments like, "No frickin' way he could have shot that number! Impossible. No frickin' way!" You catch wind of complex conspiracy theories involving certain 9-handicappers winning member-guest tournaments, or some charlatans playing on the professional mini-tours, or of the Original Sin, falsifying a handicap certificate.

25

Keep in mind that none of these alleged shenanigans will earn you a dime in prize money. If you're lucky, you might win a set of head covers. Still, given an opportunity to whine, golfers will do so with an enthusiasm matched only by multimillionaire tennis players protesting a line call.

Much of the character assassination occurs at the World's Largest 19th Hole, at the Myrtle Beach Convention Center, to which the World Ammy field repairs each night. There the participants avail themselves of perhaps the two loveliest words in the hacker's vocabulary aside from "under par." That would be "open bar." And free ribs. And countless opportunities to ogle golf products and play golf simulators and enter golf prize drawings. This nightly 19th Hole is to a 50.6-year-old 14.25-handicapper what Paris is to a lover of stinky cheese.

The only disheartening aspect of the 19th Hole, the one thing that might chase you away from all those free ribs and putting contests and jovial camaraderie, is having your score posted on a huge board, where 3,900 other sod-diggers can see it. Unless, of course, you happen to be one of those slimy low-lifes who shoots a net 58.

During the second round, at a goofy course called Brick Landing, I hit very few greens and make very few putts, which is a wonderful way to score 85. Still, after two rounds I'm tied for 30th in my flight, which should give you some idea of the general caliber of play. On one par-4 hole, my foursome scores respectively 9, 8, 6, and 6, proving incontrovertibly why the World Ammy is a *handicap* tournament. Though I cannot speak for my cohorts, whose golf demons are theirs alone to exorcise, I could offer any number of plausible excuses why I don't play stellar golf, among them tendinitis in my right elbow, which seems like the most plausible thing I can make up at this moment. Alcohol, I assure you, cannot be blamed. Mike, my playing partner from Indiana, plays miserably for approximately 12 holes, at which point he consumes three beers in a 10-minute period and pars in. Go figure.

That evening at the 19th Hole, Dr. Bob Rotella, the Tony

Robbins of golf, gives a seminar stressing the three crucial elements of golf and, subordinately, of life: the physical, mental, and spiritual. Deep stuff. The best-selling author stresses indifference and equanimity, a mind-set the dwindling crowd wandering off in search of free food seems to find at the bottom of little cups previously filled with complimentary vodka. Dr. Bob urges the hackers to dream, to imagine, to visualize their triumphs, which, to most of these guys, inspires visions of debauchery at one of Myrtle Beach's fine strip joints.

With Rotellaesque thoughts bathing my brain, I shoot a solid 40-41 at Wild Wing's Wood Stork course, tying one of the second-round leaders. Naturally, I feel pretty great, despite my requisite double-bogey or two. What's strange—and vaguely troubling—is that I play even better after the official tournament rounds, when a gang of us gathers on one of Myrtle Beach's 90 other golf courses, where we do some serious gambling. This phenomenon, I think, proves that playing for money means withstanding a little pressure, while playing for the World Ammy championship—and some head covers—is more stress than I can handle. Besides, did I mention my tendinitis?

The night before the fourth round finds the 19th Hole curiously empty. Most of the Ammies have retired early to get in touch with their indifference. Or to get a good table at the topless bar. I attend a seminar by Dave Pelz, Mr. Short Game, who helps me realize I need to start practicing my putting about six hours a day.

My last round is at Deer Track, where I shoot an inept 87, which leaves me tied for 35th. There are many good reasons why I don't shoot 79, why I don't come remotely close to winning the World Ammy, but I can't remember what they are just now. For the time being we'll stick with the tendinitis. In the elbow. Which, I would like to stress, is a very important body part when it comes to golf.

About my final round as a World Ammy participant, I want to be equanimous. I want to be indifferent. I want to be spiritual. But the truth is, I hate the greens; I hate the fairways; I hate the tee boxes; and I hate my golf game. Dr. Bob would not, I imagine, approve of my attitude. But there's something depressing about not being in contention, not being in the heat of the hunt. You get stuck in an existential bog, the links-born angst of being handicapped, of needing help, of not being able to shoot par even with help!

The beauty of the World Ammy is that approximately 3,900 other hackers feel the same. Yet one of them goes home with a big trophy and a set of head covers anyway.

4

HACKER'S HEAVEN

Payne Stewart is patrolling the practice range at Angel Park, an Arnold Palmer-designed 36-hole golf complex on the outskirts of Las Vegas. Already this November morning, he's taken a few dozen warm-up swings, pelting a defenseless flag 120 yards away with balls from identical fluid strokes of his pitching wedge. Clad in his familiar knickers and cap—today it's fetching baby blue—he stands out from the other 30 or so golfers on the range like Shaquille O'Neal in a crowd of jockeys, a virtuoso among dilettantes.

The hackers around him send sod flying, spraying hooks and slices in every direction. They know Payne Stewart—U.S. Open and Ryder Cup Champion Payne Stewart—is walking around, watching.

One 40ish gentleman, clearly an accomplished amateur, blasts ball after ball directly toward an elevated green in the distance. Payne stops behind him. "The dreaded straight ball," he says in a drawl that's part Missouri, part Texas, and part a decade and a half spent south of the Mason-Dixon on the PGA Tour.

The straight-shooting amateur, a high-ranking executive with the Prime Ticket sports television network, does his best to appear nonchalant. "Yeah, but I'd really like to hit a draw."

"Well, all right, let's see what we can do."

For the next 30 minutes, Payne Stewart coaches, cajoles, and comforts his impromptu student, adjusting his posture, fiddling with his tempo, moving his feet. He even lends him his 7-iron. A gallery of onlookers gathers, and by the end of the private lesson they're applauding the amateur's graceful gently bending golf shots. "Anything else we can do for you?" Stewart asks, grinning contentedly.

Moving down the line of turf-pounders, he's intercepted by the actor Robert Colbert, a gregarious Santa Claus of a man, Falstaffian in stature and spirit. (His encyclopedic business card bills him as, among other things, "Inventor," "Philosopher," "Sex Therapist"—"Problems Solved, Computers Tamed, Spirits Lifted, Governments Run.") Colbert extends his hand. "Mr. Stewart," he says in a stentorian baritone, "I've been waiting most of my adult life for this moment."

"Well, I'm pleased to meet you, too," Payne Stewart says, slightly abashed. "How you hittin' 'em?"

Following a brief discussion about the merits of various swing styles, Colbert strikes two gorgeous shots, both of which land within 10 feet of their target, 150 yards away.

In mock exasperation, Stewart whines, "Well, what do you want me to do? There's nothing wrong with those swings!"

"Thank you," Colbert intones, nodding his head. "Thank you. I've got something special to tell my grandchildren."

At the far end of the practice range, similar scenes are being played out between Tom Kite and an oilman from Texas; Lanny Wadkins and the owner of a Silicon Valley software company; and Davis Love III and an attorney from Chicago. Approximately four dozen American golf fanatics (and one golf-crazed Canadian), spanning the economic spectrum from the very well-off to the extremely well-off, have paid $25,000 to attend the first-ever Fantasy Golf Camp, where, if only for a few glorious days, they'll stop being CEOs and Presidents and Heads of This and That and become simply One of the Gang.

That the Gang includes some of the most illustrious golfers in the world, the incomprehensibly skillful professionals that we mortal duffers simultaneously worship and despise and envy because we never ever will play the game as well as they do—well, that's a club anyone who's ever missed a birdie putt would want to belong to.

Fantasy Golf Camp was conceived by a disparate group that includes marketers and media consultants, the agency that negotiates endorsement deals for the Tour's caddies, and Pros, Inc., the Virginia-based company that represents some of the sport's biggest celebrities. According to the founders, they envisioned the camp as a forum where, like fantasy baseball, basketball, and football camps, high-handicap hackers could play (and socialize) with their big-hitting heroes.

But unlike, say, baseball camps, Fantasy Golf has a profound resonance. Campers here are not so much trying to recapture a fondly remembered past; they're attempting to magnify the present.

Whereas most 50-year-old men—or 40- or 30-year-olds, for that matter—don't regularly don batting helmets and enjoy a rousing afternoon of brush-back fastballs and head-first dives into second base, many millions still sate their appetites for athletic competition on the genteel links. They secretly dream of getting their games in shape for the Senior Tour; they wonder what it might be like to have a grizzled yardage-quoting caddy hand them their putters and say, "That trophy's going to look awful nice over your fireplace"; and they fantasize about being on a first-name basis with the greats of the game.

"We wanted to make the fantasy a reality," the camp's founders say.

This particular reality includes a suite at Caesars Palace, limousines to and from Angel Park, meals at Spago and The Palm, a new set of Hogan clubs (in a customized Tour-style bag), the services of a PGA Tour caddie, clothes, hats, balls, tees—and lessons from, competition against, and general fraternization with a dozen or so of the sunburned magicians we watch on television every weekend.

Former Ryder Cup Captain Lanny Wadkins says that his week at Fantasy Golf Camp feels entirely different than the average Pro-Am event, where corporate honchos pay thousands of dollars to play a single round with their idols. "This is your classic Walter Mitty experience," Wadkins says, shortly before conducting a long-iron clinic. "Unlike the Pro-Am, this week I'm more interested in *their* game than mine."

Tom Kite, who was instrumental in seeing the camp through its formative stages, concurs: "At a Pro-Am, you shake hands on the first tee, play for four hours, shake hands when it's over, and say goodbye. The Pro-Am is very often my only practice round, so I can't devote much time to the guys in my group. Here, they've got us all day—and most of the night! It's a great opportunity for us to demonstrate that the people who say [tour players] have 'no personality' are dead wrong."

While the instruction at Fantasy Golf Camp is extraordinary—where else in a single morning can you get driving lessons from two-time National Long Drive Champ Art Sellinger, short-game tips from Peter Jacobsen, and putting tutelage from Steve Pate?—the campers are most excited merely to shmooze with their heroes. Whether they're John Malone's chief deputy at TCI or the president of Columbia Pictures Television, the biggest Budweiser distributor in Northern California or the Man Who Gave Mike Milken His First Job at Drexel Burnham, their glee is obvious. "I'd give up half of my company to play like them," one camper says. Standing on the tee box with John Daly as he crushes one of his frighteningly large drives (and then reports, "That was about three-quarters!") or having Davis Love peering over their shoulders, reading the break of their putts, tends to reduce the Captains of Industry to goggle-eyed awestruck teenyboppers.

And they're not ashamed to admit it. "My group played

the Scramble tournament with Lanny Wadkins today!" Brendan Murphy, a real-estate developer, gushes to a rapt smiling audience of fellow campers at dinner. "I hit a really good drive, really boomed it, and then my second shot to the green ended up about three feet from the pin—I mean, it was even closer than Lanny's!—and he says to me, 'Hey, how long have you been playing golf?' and I say, 'Seventeen months, which is the honest truth, and he says, 'Bullshit you have! You play too good.' *Lanny Wadkins* said that to me!"

One of Murphy's dining companions, another suzerain of finance who routinely closes deals valued somewhere in the neighborhood of Sri Lanka's GNP, says, "Isn't it amazing when John Daly remembers you by name? This morning he said to me, 'Hey, how you doing?' And a bunch of us were putting with him on the practice green when our round was over. For quarters. With John Daly!"

Of all the pros, Daly, the tempestuous and awesomely powerful bad boy of golf, excites the audience of millionaires the most. Yes, they may have yachts and jets and several homes in the country, but no material thing seems to thrill them quite as much as one of Daly's personalized Arkansas Razorback golf balls, which the young pro doles out to his admirers as though they were nickels.

Perhaps it's merely his astounding length, or his grip-it-and-rip-it ethos, or just his rebel-with-a-bad-haircut naughtiness that speaks so deeply to the average golfer. Whatever the source, he holds an Elvis-like sway over the campers. During one of Daly's brief visits to the practice tee, a crowd of campers gathers behind him as he launches range balls in the general direction of Arizona and the moon's gravitational field. Several football fields away, a few unsuspecting locals are working on their chipping. Like jovial children at a parade, the crowd of campers watches each of Daly's shots take flight, and then with all their lung power yell, "Fore!" at the duffers in the distance. Then they fall into hysterics.

When the pros first meet the campers in a lavish

33

Rainmanesque hospitality suite, according to Kite, "We want them to see we're just regular guys." After less than 48 hours at Fantasy Golf Camp, no one in attendance has the slightest doubt.

Whether listening to Howard Twitty recount his early years on the Asian Tour in Malaysia, where he had to kill a cobra in his golf bag with a swift swing of his 1-iron ("And that's a difficult club to hit!") or touring Las Vegas' notorious topless bars with a well-known pro who shall remain nameless here, the campers generally behave like frat boys during rush week. Even the sole female attendee, Brenda Markstein, a 7-handicap grandmother whose husband gave her Fantasy Golf Camp as a birthday present, insists she just wants to be one of the guys. Except most of the guys wish they played as well as the gal. Instead, they must content themselves with drinking contests against NBC commentator Gary Koch, invading the blackjack tables with Blaine McCallister, and setting Wolfgang Puck's tablecloth on fire during drinks at Spago.

The week's unofficial Course Jester, and possibly the most enthusiastic camper, is Vegas artifact and inveterate divot-maker Buddy Hackett, who offers a driving tip to John Daly: "You're too sober!" To Payne Stewart he recounts: "I was playing golf the other day and a Japanese guy says to me, 'Pray faster! Pray faster!' I says to him, 'You know, I really enjoyed killing your uncle.' Jap says to me, 'When, in World War Two?' 'No,' I says, 'Last week on the golf course, when he told me to pray faster!'"

When he's not imploring Mark Carnevale or Mike Standly to watch his 150-yard drives ("Didja see that?!"), Buddy has a habit of announcing to no one in particular, "This is the greatest golf experience of my life." Funny thing is, everyone else is saying the same thing.

Maybe it's because the pros are treating this week not as a lark, but as though it were another crucial date on their perpetual Tour. Davis Love admits, "It's hard to be the guy everyone is all excited about. Expectations are very high." Lanny Wadkins claims, "I feel a lot of pressure to play well during a week like this. Really, I do." And Tom Kite (former all-time leading money winner Tom Kite) says, "I definitely feel a twinge of nervousness when I'm playing a scramble with [the campers] and it comes down to me making a key shot. If you're a competitor, you care."

For all the unbridled idol worship that occurs during a Fantasy Golf Camp, after a few days of relentless intimacy with the great ones, the campers feel comfortable enough to actually *needle* the best golfers in the world—and how often does a double-digit-handicap get to heckle a guy who's earned gazillions on the golf course? When Tom Kite "tees off" for the Fantasy Golf Camp's putting tournament, played on Angel Park's exquisitely cruel miniature course, everyone there knows he's generally considered one of the most consistent putters in the game. So when his first putt dribbles meekly down a slope and into a "fairway" bunker, the taunts of "Hit it, Alice!" and "Girlie Man!" could probably be heard all the way to the Strip. And when Tom Kite—*Tom Kite*, for crissakes—takes *five* strokes to get down on this par-3 70-foot hole, all the hopeless hackers in attendance who managed to make better than double-bogey (and even those who didn't) howl like jackals, telling Kite he ought to be assessed a slow-play penalty and, by the way, would he like some lessons?

Kite runs through the stock gestures of disappointment: the grimace, the head shake, the silently mouthed curse, the hands on hips, the long exhale. And then he smiles. He knows that for a fleeting seldom repeated moment he has played a hole of golf as badly as everyone else. He knows that four dozen campers are going to return home and tell anyone who'll listen how they bettered Tom Kite in a putting competition. He knows that, if only for a moment, he's made a lot of fantasies come true.

5

THE NEED
FOR SPEED

While playing in the British Isles not long ago, I came upon a funny sign posted on the first tee of a seaside course. "Gentlemen, please play quickly!" the sign implored. "Four hours is too long for a round of golf!"

Imagine such a sign in America, home of the motorized cart and six-hour traffic jams. These days a four-hour round on the home turf is about as rare as a double eagle.

Slow play is strangling our beloved game. It's robbing participants of enjoyment, course owners of revenue, and families of their moms and dads. ("Don't worry, sweetheart. I know she's been away since dawn, but Mommy will be home from the golf course by nightfall, I promise.") What used to be a morning's preamble or an afternoon's getaway has devolved into an entire day's commitment—and most people can't afford to invest a whole day digging up sod.

Almost no one follows the pace-of-play guidelines that many public courses print on their scorecards. The prevailing attitude seems to be, "I paid my damned green fee. I'm gonna play from whatever damned tees I want and as slow as I damned please." Thus, course rangers (or "player assistants," as they're euphemistically known) are helpless. How can they identify the slow-playing culprits when nearly everyone on the course is getting his "money's worth"?

I know more than a few disconsolate hackers who have quit the game out of frustration. Golf, they realized, just takes too long.

If you're one of them, or in danger of becoming so, it might cheer you to know that when a San Diego resident named Jay Larson plays golf, he usually scores in the 70s. It might cheer you even more to know that he scores in the 70s and doesn't need anything like six hours to do it.

In fact, in his last officially timed round, on a 6,200-yard course (about 3.5 miles), he shot 76. And it took him exactly 39 minutes, 39 seconds.

He doesn't use a cart, rocket-powered or otherwise; he doesn't skip holes; and he definitely doesn't stand over shots, going through a 24-point checklist of swing thoughts. He just plays golf really, really fast.

Jay Larson is the world's number-one-ranked player in speed golf. Formerly known as "xtreme golf," speed golf, like the Olympic biathlon, is a hybrid of two pure sports: distance running and golf. Players compete in time trials that work like this: You hit your ball, you run to it, you hit it again. When you've completed 18 holes, you're done.

Your score is figured by adding your elapsed time to the number of strokes. (For example, someone who takes 90 minutes and shoots 80 has scored 170 in speed golf.) Caddies, who use a cart, are allowed; pouting, whining, and mulligans are not.

"This game is the difference between a sport and a pastime," Larson explains. "Speed golf is an opportunity to play golf in a more athletic way. And," he says, laughing, "a lot faster."

This sport favors the physically fit. Most PGA Tour celebrities—with the exception of David Duval, whose workout regimen is legendary—would finish well back in the pack in a speed golf event. Jack Nicklaus, the father of slow play, and Tiger Woods, his heir, might not even make the cut.

❖ ❖ ❖

Jay Larson, 42, looks a little like Nick Nolte—if Nick Nolte ran 50 miles a week. Larson is long and thin, with the easy loping stride of a seasoned runner. Which he is. In fact, Jay Larson is a former professional triathlete, a two-time finisher of the Ironman World Championship in Hawaii (he finished 11th in his first try), who was once ranked as high as eighth in the world. But previous to running, biking, and swimming unfathomable distances in unfathomably fast times, he was a PGA professional, a protegé of the late Senior Tour star Larry Gilbert. Larson played the mini-tours and knocked around at club jobs in the Los Angeles area before answering the siren call of carbo-loading and oxygen debt. Burned out on marathon running by the age of 33, Larson returned to golf in his mid-30s and immediately started scoring in the 60s.

Around that time, America's most famous miler, Steve Scott, set a "world record" for a round of golf—though making a good score wasn't a consideration. (He shot 98 in around 29 minutes.) "I got jealous," Larson recalls. "I wanted to break that record."

In 1994 he got his chance. Larson was invited to an organized speed golf tournament, one that uses the sport's current scoring formula. On a 6,600-yard course with a 125 slope rating, he shot a 75 in 39 minutes. For the next four years, he won every speed golf event he entered, earning the unofficial honorific, "World's Fastest Golfer."

Last summer, he started organizing and promoting speed golf events. His governing body, the World Speed Golf Association, dropped the word "xtreme," since, to the 40-year-olds this sport seems to attract, "xtreme" means switching from balata to Surlyn. "The only thing extreme about this sport is that we're extremely interested in picking up the pace of play," Larson says. "In every other way we play a very traditional game of golf." Indeed, speed golf players adhere to all but two USGA rules: leaving the flagstick in on putts and not requiring lost balls to be played from where they were originally struck. "Our sport is about freeing up your mind and body. That's about as radical as we get."

The first speed golf event Larson managed was the first one he ever lost, finishing second to Dave Aznavorian, a marketing manager for Titleist golf clubs, who shot a two-over 74 in 38:11. Having had the pleasure of playing (regular golf) with the Az, I can vouch for his golf skills. But 38:11? That's about how long it takes most of us duffers to play three holes, two on a slow day. "I'm a serious 'ten-K' runner," Aznavorian says. "This isn't for everyone. But speed golf is a perfect combination for me."

To keep up with the Az and other speedy competitors, Larson trains assiduously, playing "regular golf" at a sloth-like 3½ hour pace and doing endless miles of road work. Always looking for ways to cut seconds off his game, Larson is trying to shrink his "pre-shot routine" from about seven seconds to five. "That's over thirty seconds a round right there," he explains.

He invites me to join him on one of his informal training rounds, which typically take place before sensible people have rolled out of bed. When the sun peeks above the horizon, Larson is off and running—and swinging, and running. "We'll probably be finished with our round before the first regular group has played four holes," he predicts.

I join Larson at the Lomas Santa Fe golf course, near Del Mar, California, where he's promised to initiate me into the ways of high-speed hacking. Though it's only an "executive" layout—about 2,200 yards, mostly par-3s—I'm nervous about trying to make decent golf swings while running about a mile and a half. "Do you play better in three hours or five?" Larson asks rhetorically. "Sports are about rhythm. *Everything* in life is about rhythm. Slow golf steals that aspect from the game."

For the sake of speed, he recommends I wear running shoes instead of spikes, eschew practice swings, take no time to read putts—"When in doubt, hit it straight!" he advises—and, above all, forget about posing after a sweetly struck tee shot. "You definitely want to be running while the ball is still in the air," Larson counsels.

The first hole is a downhill 160-yard par-3. With enough

adrenaline coursing through me to light the Vegas Strip, I send my ball skyward and take off at close to a full sprint. Predictably, I arrive greenside with the kind of accelerated heart rate that discourages genteel putting strokes. At this torrid pace, I'll either shatter all the speed golf records or end up in the San Diego cardiac unit. After 3-putting through tear-filled eyes, I realize I'd better drop the journalist-impersonating-a-Kenyan-miler routine in favor of a sensible jog through the park.

Settling into a comfortable pace, I begin to strike the ball cleanly and crisply, propelling it in the general direction it's meant to go. There's no time to think about anything, and after playing analytical reflective golf for most of my life, I begin to believe that thoughtlessness might be a good thing. Speed golf is very Zen. The only problem, I discover, is putting: I'm all jacked up on lactic acid, so nearly all my first putts end up at least three or four feet past the hole. Strangely, the come-backers, over which I'd normally agonize, all seem to end up in the bottom of the cup. Speed golf doesn't leave time for the yips.

It takes me seven holes before I record my first par of the round. At first blush that seems pretty sad. But here's another way of looking at it: My first par comes less than 12 minutes after my opening tee shot.

In fact, I complete my entire round in 25 minutes.

Drenched with perspiration and mildly winded, I tally up the damage: I've played slightly worse than bogey golf. This isn't unusual for me. I'm thoroughly capable of making a bad score any time I play. I can shoot bogey golf or worse at will.

But it usually takes me five hours to do it.

6

WIZARDS
OF THE WAND

Putting a golf ball is not, as cliché-mongers say, brain surgery. Though both activities require the use of specialized instruments (scalpels; Wilson 8802 blades) and fine motor skills under immense pressure, brain surgery, let's face it, requires slightly more training. Putting is to athletics what microwaving a package of frozen lasagna is to gastronomy. To be a good putter, you don't have to be a good athlete. You don't even have to be a good golfer. You've just got to be able to roll a golf ball into a hole using a mallet on a stick. Any fat, out-of-shape, 36-handicapper can do it. Even a fat, out-of-shape, dilettante journalist can do it.

On occasion.

Of course, there are times when even the best putters among us *can't* do it. Which shows, I think, that putting is not so much a physical skill as it is a mental thing, just as dementia is a mental thing.

Now, the reason I'm writing this story instead of sitting in a lounge chair overlooking the Monterey Peninsula with a comely lass by my side, a tall drink in one hand, and, in the other, the $250,000 I have won for placing first in the Compaq World Putting Championship by Dave Pelz is because I didn't win the Compaq World Putting Championship by Dave Pelz.

It's that whole mental-thing business.

❖ ❖ ❖

Let me explain the various components of the phrase "Compaq World Putting Championship by Dave Pelz": "Compaq" is the large, Texas-based, computer company, which paid what I assume to be a commensurately large fee to be the title sponsor of the event; "World Putting Championship" is a two-day tournament in which amateur state putting champions, PGA club professionals, touring PGA, Senior PGA, and LPGA professionals—and the odd golf writer—attempt to perform a ridiculously simple physical task without suffering a complete collapse of their central nervous systems; "Dave Pelz," America's foremost authority on the short game, devised the three putting games used to determine the world's greatest putter.

Those would be: "Drawback," in which all missed putts are "drawn back" 34 inches (about the length of a standard putter) until you hole out; "Safety Drawback," in which all missed putts are drawn back except those that finish in a 34-inch "safe zone" behind the hole; and "Double Safety Drawback," in which all missed putts not in the safe zone are drawn back 68 inches. The purpose of Pelz's putting games is to test all aspects of putting skills, including lag-putting, green-reading, and the ability to sink those dreaded four-footers.

Like an intemperate college boy cramming for the Psych 101 final he's been avoiding all semester in favor of 99-cent draft specials, I spend most of the night before the first round of the World Putting Championship putting on my hotel carpet. I do this not only because, in a fit of sudden self-knowledge, I realize I have not practiced nearly enough for this event, but also because, I tell myself, "Hey, putting on your hotel carpet! Cool! That's what the pros do on the eve of the final round."

Obviously, I do not sleep. Instead I divine subtle "breaks" in the shadows on the ceiling.

When morning finally comes, I hurry to the Bonnet

Creek golf complex at daybreak. When I arrive, 100 bleary-eyed putters are already there.

❖ ❖ ❖

Faced with an enormous challenge that instills a mixture of fright and longing in their bellies, most people take the slightest occurrence as a momentous sign. They get superstitious. Miss the first nine putts of the day and, well, it's clear that It Just Wasn't Meant To Be. Make two six-footers in a row and an Odyssey endorsement deal beckons. I tell myself I will not partake of such nonsense. I vow I will be, Susan Sontag-like, against interpretation. I pledge to be strong.

Then I make two six-footers in a row and become as superstitious as a conspiracy theorist finding hidden messages spelled out in the curls of Chelsea Clinton's hair.

It's a mental thing.

My first-round playing partner is LPGA pro Cindy Schreyer, who is as sweet, supportive, and genial as any trembling amateur could wish. Her good nature calms me. Perhaps even more important is my bliss-breeding ignorance: When we commence our round, I'm not aware that Miss Schreyer is the second-ranked putter on the LPGA Tour.

Our initial game is Double Safety Drawback, the most difficult of Pelz's formats, where most of your second putts are seven to ten feet. Miraculously, I make only one 4-putt while sinking a couple of slam-dunk aces and shoot a respectable 4-over 22, besting my professional partner by two strokes. Staunchly in the middle of the pack after the first nine holes, I am more relieved and amazed than jubilant and eager.

In the second round, playing Drawback, we both putt well, carding 2-over 20s. My 6-over total after 18 holes is good for 22nd place in the field of 163. For a time I'm actually able to enjoy myself. I note the ESPN cameras, the modest gallery, the "Quiet, Please!" sign-toting marshals. And I whisper, "Hey, this is *cool*," before I catch myself sounding like Beavis and Butthead.

Strolling off the putting green—okay, perhaps *strutting* is more like it—I have somehow convinced myself that I actually belong here in the World Putting Championship. (This is a complicated process involving the repetition of reassuring mantras like, "You can really putt/You can really putt," and the proper reading of momentous signs.) Regrettably, a midday lunch break gives me far too much time to ponder scenarios and propositions I've not yet dared to entertain except in my most psychotic moments. Such as: I could actually make the cut and get in the finals!

I do not enjoy lunch.

Round three is the easiest game, Safety Drawback, and I know I should be able to move up the leaderboard. Instead, I become intensely aware of the ESPN cameras, the modest gallery, the sign-toting marshals—not to mention the beating of my heart, which I sometimes think I can hear as I stand over a downhill left-to-right 12-footer. I shoot a disastrous, 5-over 23.

Now I'm around 50th place. Sixty-one players will make the first-day cut and move into the finals to face the exempt world-famous players. I tell myself I have nine holes left to discover my destiny. And then I realize I don't even believe in things like destiny. Needing to make a few putts has turned me into a fateful Calvinist, like an agnostic converted on his deathbed. If my throat weren't so dry, I would laugh at myself.

Apparently, all the moisture in my body has collected in my palms, which are so slick I can barely grip my old, beat-up Delta 145 putter. I immediately 3- and 4-putt the first two holes of the last nine.

Motivated now by rage—at myself, for letting it all slip away when it was in my grasp—I play the next seven holes well, scaring the ball into the hole with an icy scowl. The turning point is 2-putting from 81 feet, the longest hole in the tournament. After snaking in a smelly five-footer at the last, I allow myself a Nicklaus-like, upraised flourish of my putter, knowing for a moment what it's like to make a putt that you really, *really* need to make.

And then I wait. My 16-over total is going to be close to the cut line.

So, like a rookie at the Tour Q-school, for 55 interminable minutes I get to experience something nobody should ever have to endure: sweating a leaderboard. The projections keep changing: 15-over; 17-over; 18-over; 17-over. Not knowing (or caring) if I am betraying the spirit of Old Tom Morris and beautiful Bobby Jones, I find myself silently rooting for lots of high scores. Now, whether this makes me a bad person—or a bad golfer—I'm not sure. Of this, however, I am certain: Sweating leaderboards week after week on Tour is no way to make a living.

After the last scores are posted, it's official: I'm in by one stroke. I'm in the finals.

I would probably cry tears of joy if all my body's salty fluids hadn't already escaped through the pores in my hands. Instead, I do what I imagine all the pros do: say some gracious thank you's, have a glass of wine, and retire to the hotel room for an evening of putting on the carpet.

❖ ❖ ❖

The next morning, surveying the practice putting green filled with superstars whose exploits I have spent many of my working days chronicling, I feel excited, yet at the same time strangely placid, as though I'm enveloped by some sort of *Golf in the Kingdom* purple energy cocoon. Either that or I had slightly too much wine last night. There's Payne Stewart. There's Bob Murphy. And over there, Tom Kite and Andy North are chatting with Brad Faxon and Beth Daniel.

And the great thing is, armed with my official contestant's money clip, I don't have to stop outside the gallery ropes and watch. I can go putt with them. Which I do. All the U.S. Open champs are sort of watching but not really watching. Still, my warm-up goes well, which I conveniently take to be a *very good* sign.

When the pairings are announced, I'm thrilled to learn that I'll be playing with another U.S. Open champ, Lee Janzen. Kite is in the group ahead of me and Faxon, generally considered one of the best putters on the PGA Tour, is in the group behind me. Now I know I really don't belong.

On the first hole, playing Double Safety Drawback, the hardest game, I'm faced with a slippery eight-footer for par and coolly roll it in. "Nice putt," Lee Janzen says. For a millisecond I think, "Lee Janzen just said 'Nice putt' to me." But despite the cameras, and the now sizable gallery, and the proximity to major-championship winners and a Ryder Cup captain—despite everything that ought to be making me a wreck, I feel good. I feel confident. I feel like I can putt.

My respectable 3-over 21 beats Mr. Janzen by three strokes and Mr. Faxon by five.

On the second nine my sterling play continues. In between lighthearted chats with Mr. Kite and Mr. Stewart, I sink my first ace of the finals and leave another one on the lip. I feel like I'm in a highly improbable movie, the kind where you know you're headed for a deliriously happy ending, but you watch anyway, because that's exactly what you want to happen. I shoot a 1-over 19, my best round of the week. My 4-over total puts me solidly in the top 20. If I have a fair, just a slightly below average, final nine holes, I'll make the 40-player cut and participate in a putt-off for the quarter-million.

❖ ❖ ❖

Did I mention that putting is a mental thing?

On the final nine holes I choke. I crumble. I disintegrate.

My breath gets quick, my stroke is poor, and my results are predictable. With every 3-putt—and there are many of them—I see my destiny falling like a soufflé in the payload of a pickup truck. It's like being in a car wreck, knowing that the big truck veering into your lane is going to slam into you and you're powerless to stop it. Janzen, befitting a champion, makes everything he looks at and sneaks into the money round. I shoot an 8-over 26 and miss the final cut by two strokes. My putter is a sword, and I have fallen upon it.

Back on the sidelines, with notebook in hand, I make the depressing transition from Player to Member of the Media. Watching Len Mattiace, a PGA Tour player, win the $250,000, I'm filled with the kind of bleak, dull sickness you feel when you've awakened from a magnificent dream, only to realize it's been a magnificent dream. No, I am not the Best Putter on Earth. But, then, neither is Brad Faxon, who not only didn't make the cut, but also suffered the unspeakable indignity of finishing one stroke behind a lowly golf writer.

I console myself with such facts. I remind myself that while I am not the Best Putter, not even close, until next year's Compaq World Putting Championship by Dave Pelz comes around, I can say I am the 57th best putter in the world.

And sometimes, when the whole mental thing is working right, I'll even believe it.

7

ON MASHIE! ON NIBLICK! ON SPOONIE! ON STYMIE! 'TIS THE HOLIDAY SEASON: NOW, WHAT WILL YOU BUY ME?

'Twas the night before Christmas
When all through the land,
Not a golfer was putting—
They were all in the sand.
"More distance! More hang-time! More pars!" they did clamor.
"Please sell us equipment that allows us to hammer
Our balls down the fairways and straight to the greens!
Make us Norman-like, Pavinesque birdie machines!"

The golf biz responded with typical vigor,
Selling balls, clubs, and gee-gaws to withstand the rigor
Of millions of hackers digging the sod,
Searching for sweet spots, salvation, and God.
Top-Flite and Titleist, Cobra and Ping—
All purvey the goods that make duffers' hearts sing:
"Oversized," "cavity-backed," "lighter and stronger,"
All manners of magic to shoot straighter and longer.

Our handicaps stay on the loftiest plane.
But still we play on, ignoring the pain,
The indignity, the comedy, the sheer foolishness,
The pathos, the pity, the rank ghoulishness
Of toying with clubs that cost as much as a grand,
Yet posting a score far higher than planned.

"You'll play better golf," the marketers crow.
A fair trade-off, we think, for spending such dough.
Still, year after year, when December rolls 'round,
We search high and low and discover we've found
Improvements minute and our charge card bills higher—
Fine reason, we think, to quit and retire.

But each autumn in Vegas, 'fore the holiday season,
The PGA Golf Show provides us a reason
To shop and to buy and, bedazzled again,
To think that we're players—not mere mortal men.
With over 900 booths luring us near,
If this were a mountain, they'd call it Mount Gear.

I roamed the convention floor, traversed the aisles,
Looking at golf stuff that spread out for miles.
A sound swing, I noticed, was never for sale,
But you could find comp'nies to tell you a tale
Of fresh innovations to make you play better,
Like Davies and Pepper and lovely Kris Tschetter.
A bevy of products, so much that's brand-new,
There's only the space here to speak of a few.
The choice in the end, oh consumer, it's yours.
So dream of yourself in some spanking plus fours.
I can't guarantee that a club oversize
Will send your ball winging the length of the skies,
But come Christmas night, when you're full of the Yule,
Whatever your talent, at least you'll look cool.

Tommy Armour's Ti 100, the largest of large,
Is so mammothly sized it will give you a charge.
The ball near the club looks as small as a marble.
But, as they say down in Dixie, you still might play "harrble."
How could I make bogeys with clubs of titanium?
So vexing this quandary, it tortures the cranium.

Other comp'nies are using the metal as well,
Though only as inserts, which is not quite as swell.

The payoff, they claim, is perimeter weighting,
Which should have your drives on more fairways awaiting.
Your mis-hits, you see, the rationale goes,
Feel better when hit off the heel or the toe
Or the shaft or the grip or anyplace else
For those times when you're swinging unlike young Ernie Els.

Upon reaching your ball, you'll employ with esprit
More clubs for the bag: Mizuno's T-Zoid T-3,
Top-Flite's Tour Ti, Powerbilt's TPS Ti
All promise (in writing) to make your ball fly!
The mass is increased around the club's head,
Yet these spatula irons aren't heavy as lead.
They're light and they're soft and they hit it a mile.
And holy aesthetics! They're crafted with style,
Looking good in your hands and when addressing the ball.
So good, in fact, you won't mind it at all
That suggested retail on a set of these honeys
Is close to $1,000—no small sum of monies.

Some of the biggest have brought out new lines
For those "better players" who appreciate signs
Of traditional clubs that are neither too big nor small,
Not too fancy or wide, not too short or too tall.
You won't find titanium in these new sticks,
But that doesn't mean they're intended for hicks.
Taylor Made has the Burner Tour Irons, a blade
Neither stuffy nor stodgy nor especially staid.
It features the brand's famous black shaft of bubble,
Whose lower center of gravity should keep you from trouble.
These good-looking clubs are meant to send your ball steamin':
Just ask British Open Champ (and paid endorser) Tom Lehman.
The esteemed brand of Dunlop is back with an iron,
The Tour DG series, which will have aces firin'
Over hazards and bunkers and straight at the pin,
Like Faldo, Montgomerie, and champ Lee Janzen.
These clubs feel like a forge, though they're really a cast.
Their True Temper EI shaft lets you swing smooth, not fast.

I played a round with these babes and they sure felt good,
Even when I swung as hard as I could.
For those who want clubs that feel caressingly soft,
Try Dunlop's RMS in all types of lofts.
(Resonance Modulation System is tough;
As a rhyme it's a ball buried deep in the rough.)
It's called a "balata club," with a soft plastic ring
That dampens impact and lessens the sting
Of off-center slices and wicked duck hooks,
Which everyone hits—even sniper Mark Brooks.

Ferralium 255 is the metal at Lynx,
Whose Black Cat Tour iron strokes feral, me thinks.
Eastwood, Nicholson, Lampley, and Nantz are all owners
Of this celebrity-packed company looking for donors.
That would be you and that would be me:
The golf-crazed hacks who are hoping to see
Their scores go from bogeys and in some cases doubles
To the numbers produced by McGann and Fred Couples.

There's Cobra's King Cobra II. Its "IQ" system
Has alleged benefits: I can try here to list 'em.
The clubs are supposed to expose the sweet spot—
Not every so often, but shot after shot.
Employing designs that I cannot explain,
So advanced, so ingenious, I may go insane.
Deciphering the hyperscientific mumbo jumbo
Makes a poor hacker like me feel like a dumbo.

If price is no issue, then come right this way,
Up to the Ram vendors, who would like you to pay
A grand, more or less, at suggested retail
For one single golf club, perfect in detail.
It's a Ti-Forged Driver and one of a kind.
For strokes out of sight, pay a price out of mind.

Another great way to set free lots of bread,
To be as loose in the wallet as perhaps in the head,

Awaits those consumers on profligate edges.
Over $800 for a set of three wedges?
Yes. Made by Cleveland and designed by Byron and Corey,
Masters of short game—well, you know the story.
These wedges are handsome and solid as rocks.
And don't sweat the price; it includes a nice box.

The king of the price tag, for ladies or men,
Is the company within Phil Mickelson's ken.
My family will tell you—take it from the Koniks—
The highest-priced stuff is manufactured by Yonex.

I wish you good golf, now, and plenty of fun.
May your game be as smooth as Steve Elkington.
May you play as though guided by a force from above
And hit it as far as the long Davis Love.
May your holiday season be filled with good cheer.
Say, after the golf, may I buy you a beer?
To the duffers and hackers, to the sweet-swinging pros,
To all on whom this Royal & Ancient game grows:
May you live to discover equipment that's right.
To all a good round, and to all a good night!

Players
of the Game

8

A YOUNG HOGAN

Something wonderful happened on the PGA Tour in 1997: A bunch of wildly talented kids stormed the old-guard professional golf world, like so many range balls raining down on a defenseless target green.

This "new breed" served notice that international tournament golf will have a fresh (and telegenic) roster of celebrities to carry the game into the 21st century, long after Arnie and Jack and Lee and Raymond and Chi-Chi have struck their last drives. In '97, Phil Mickelson won again, as he has every year since he joined the Tour. David Duval won back-to-back at the end of the season, shattering his bridesmaid syndrome that had previously soured everyone's "can't-miss" expectations. And another player in his 20s won golf's most treasured major championship.

You may have heard of this fellow. Despite his age, he's among the most respected players in the world, possessed of staggering physical talents and mental powers. If you care at all about golf, when this mere lad won his major championship, you had to find his final-round performance one of the year's most gripping athletic spectacles.

He's handsome and charismatic, and he's got the kind of elegant presence on a golf course parents should hope their children will emulate.

No, not Tiger Woods.

Justin Leonard. The defending British Open champion.

❖ ❖ ❖

It's Tuesday and sunny. The monsoon that has engulfed California for months has lifted momentarily, and the entrants in the Nissan Open, the PGA Tour's Los Angeles stop, are eager to walk in the rare sunshine. They fill the fairways of Valencia Country Club to play low-stakes practice rounds. At most Tour events, Tuesday is the best day of the week for golf fans to watch their heroes up close, before the cameras and crowds arrive later in the week. You can get close enough to hear Fred Couples chatting with Lanny Wadkins about sports, Payne Stewart consulting his caddie, or Craig Stadler sighing heavily after a wayward approach shot. Along the first hole, hundreds of awestruck admirers slosh through the muddy rough to get an intimate glimpse of Phil Mickelson and Tiger Woods, who have just teed off. Like paparazzi elbowing their way to a prime vantage point at the Academy Awards, the assertive golf fans who have worked to the front of the horde, up to the edge of the restraining yellow ropes, are rewarded with classic Tuesday action. While waiting to play their second shots, Tiger tries swinging Phil's lefty wedge, while Mike "Fluff" Cowan, Tiger's increasingly famous caddie, attempts to explain a complex mud-on-a-ball theory ("Seriously, you can predict which way it'll spit") to anyone who will listen. Tiger and Phil know that their every utterance, their every gesture, no matter how innocuous, is being consumed by a large live audience. Woods and Mickelson are both rich and famous, and they don't seem to mind that another casual Tuesday has brought them an immense gallery worthy of a final-round playoff.

Meanwhile, on the 11th fairway, exactly five people are following a trio of players, one of whom happens to be the reigning British Open champion.

Three of the fans are snowboarder dudes cutting class;

they don't know whom they're watching. The other fans are a couple of young women who have driven down from Fresno to get a peek at young Mr. Leonard, an eligible bachelor, in person. They have a bit of a crush on him. One of them, Jennifer, says, "He's like the boy next door. Very cute."

Is she aware that Tiger Woods is just a few holes away? "Sure," she says dismissively. "But his attitude makes me ill. Justin is the total opposite."

Yes, Justin Leonard is indeed cut from a different mold. He's only 26, but so much about him suggests another era, a way of playing golf—and living life—that's old-fashioned: the peculiar low-brim hat; the carefully clean-shaven neck; the strong angular facial features, borrowed, it seems, from a silent-movie hero; the meticulous Polo wardrobe; the methodical, never-changing, pre-shot routine; the purposeful walk; the focus.

During the practice round he keeps his own yardage book, making detailed notes about the greens—the way professionals played golf in bygone days. He goes about his business quietly, without a legion of followers—but he's widely admired by his fellow players, who treat him like a 20-year veteran. He was one of the last Tour players to switch to a metal driver. (Armed with persimmon, Justin seemed positively antique.) Even with all the modern newfangled technology in his bag, Justin reminds you of Ben Hogan. Like Leonard, Hogan was from the Dallas area, made practicing an informal religion, and developed an icy concentration during competition that left him seemingly immune to this thing we call pressure. It's no surprise that Justin plays Hogan-brand irons.

Justin Leonard has that kind of low constant burn, the determination of the great ones. He's perfected a sizzling stare worthy of Ray Floyd—and a game to go with it.

At 5'9", 160 pounds, Leonard is usually the short man off the tee. But he's also often the closest man on the green. "The way I grew up, playing with older kids, I had to think my way around the golf course," Justin Leonard tells me after completing his Tuesday practice round. "I had to become a good long-iron player and I had to get sharp around the greens. That's still true. A lot of guys out here hit it a long way. They play a different game than I do. But we all find a way to get the job done."

Justin has always found a way. At every stage in his golf career, he's enjoyed success. Many years ago, his agent, Mac Barnhardt, who affectionately calls his client "the kid," predicted to me that young Leonard would be something special. Mac was right. In 1992 Justin was the World Amateur of the Year and the U.S. Amateur champion. In 1994 he was the NCAA champion and *Golfweek* College Player of the Year. In 1996 he won his first PGA Tour event, the Buick Open, and earned a spot on the President's Cup team. In 1997 all he did was make the Ryder Cup squad, finish seventh in the Masters, place second at the PGA Championship and win the British Open.

"That was a lot of fun," Leonard says of his Open victory. "The final round, it was one of those days where the hole just seemed to get bigger." Were the last two holes nerve-racking, knowing he was so close to making history? "I tried to stay focused on the task, not the result. But when the result is right *there*"—he nods—"it's tough." Near the end, Bob [Riefke, his caddie] and I talked about staining his deck."

❖ ❖ ❖

Unlike his long-hitting under-30 peers, whose power amazes everyone, Justin Leonard doesn't overwhelm a golf course. He dissects it.

I ask Tiger Woods to analyze the Leonard game. "We're two totally different styles," Woods tells me, flashing his highly endorsed smile. "Justin isn't long. But he's a great grinder. He's usually hitting longer irons into greens than some guys, which can sometimes be an advantage when you want to control trajectory. And he's a great putter."

Woods has known Leonard since Tiger was 13 and Justin was 17. "During the Ryder Cup, he didn't talk at all while we were playing together. That reminded me of when we were kids," Woods recalls. "We were playing in a junior tournament in Texarkana, and he had a big lead, maybe three or four shots. I'll never forget it. I thought I could possibly catch him. No chance. He destroyed me by, like, seven shots. And he didn't talk to me the entire round back then, either. Not one word."

A straight hitter (he's typically among the Tour leaders in driving accuracy) and a terrific putter, Leonard is sharp in every aspect of the game. But his real strength, he says, is "managing myself, even when my ball-striking isn't quite there."

Growing up in Dallas, Justin Leonard played a lot of golf with his parents. "I had a little temper," he remembers, "and they quickly put me in my place. They taught me it doesn't look good, and it's not productive. I'm naturally pretty hard on myself—both on and off the course. I've learned to try to channel that energy in a way that isn't offensive or destructive."

He admits he might mutter under his breath occasionally—"I can't tell you what I say; it's not printable!" he jokes—but in general, his on-course strategy is to leave the past in the past. "I don't want to damage my confidence when I stand over my next shot," Leonard explains. "Once I make a mistake, it's over. I'm on to my next shot. I used to think about my bad shots for maybe five minutes too long. But you realize the really successful players can control themselves in tough situations."

The commissioner of the PGA Tour, Tim Finchem, echoes this sentiment: "Justin Leonard is one of those guys who you like right off the bat. He's a tremendous asset to the Tour, just the way he handles himself."

"Some of my friends say I act like I'm forty years old," Leonard admits. "I'm pretty reflective. I like to leave the golf course at the end of the day knowing I handled things as well I could."

During the British Open, Leonard's wise-beyond-his-years maturity was in evidence both in victory and defeat.

At Troon, where his stellar ball-striking and clutch putting earned him the Claret Jug, Justin accepted his triumph with a plain-spoken grace that was both moving and refreshing. After thanking the greenskeeper (!) and several British golf officials, Justin thanked his fellow competitors and his playing partner that day, Freddie Couples. Then, speaking extemporaneously about his family and their pride at his accomplishment, he had to step away from the microphones to compose himself. He seemed at that moment a tender young boy who had somehow accomplished a much older man's goal.

At Winged Foot, where Davis Love foiled Leonard's attempt at back-to-back majors, Justin proved that in this age of the bad attitude, golf can still be the domain of the gentleman. As he and Love walked up the 18th fairway, Leonard displayed the kind of sportsmanship that seems at times to have disappeared from most other professional athletics.

Reliving the walk up the 18th fairway, Leonard says, "I was disappointed to be so close. You don't get that many chances to win a major, and I let this one slip away. But my friend was so excited. A ten-year burden had been lifted. So I was feeling joy for him. I told myself I could save my disappointment for later. There would be plenty of time for that. But this was the only time to share pure joy with him," he says, shrugging. "I was so happy for Davis. And I wanted him to know that."

Justin put his arm around Davis and said as much. Millions of viewers, including myself, realized once more why they love this game.

Shortly after Leonard relates his Winged Foot anecdote, I ask Tiger if he's worked at the mental side of his game, specifically on his on-course conduct. Tiger Woods assures me that he has no plans to adjust his attitude on the golf course, that he'll be swearing and throwing clubs and calling himself "the worst golfer on the planet" his whole career. "It's a release," he explains matter-of-factly.

I realize then why millions of fans, including myself, root for a young champion named Justin Leonard.

9

THE MONEY PLAYER

They're called "money players"—the guys you would want to make a six-foot putt if your life depended on it; the gals who transform pressure into a staple of their diet; the players who aren't afraid to win.

Money players are as rare as double eagles. Occasionally, you'll find them hanging around big-city muni courses, but more often at the toniest country clubs, or in Vegas, where those with a taste for gambling tend to congregate on the fairways. Anywhere cash flows. But the truth is, you won't find many of these money players on any of the major tours. It's one thing to play for someone else's money, the hundreds of thousands (sometimes millions) of dollars supplied by market-hungry sponsors. It's another to have to dig deep into your wallet when you yip a putt on the 18th.

Lee Trevino—a money player of the highest order—said that playing professionally, in the land of courtesy cars and chartered jets, isn't pressure. Pressure, he said, is playing a ten dollar Nassau when you have only two dollars in your pocket.

The superstars of the Senior PGA Tour have considerably more than two dollars in their collective pockets. They don't lack for anything. But look around the practice tee.

Do a little survey. Ask the fellows who among their peers is a money player, the guy who stares down fear and *wills* his ball into the hole when it counts. They all mention the same man.

Which is why, when I meet Raymond Floyd on the first tee of the Dominion Country Club to join him for a round of golf, I do not ask him if he wants to play for a little something.

Floyd is in San Antonio for the Southwestern Bell Dominion, a Senior Tour stop known for its hard greens, high winds, and Tex-Mex hospitality. It's Pro-Am day, that compulsory, pre-tournament, exhibition round where golf stars and their supplicants mingle freely, trading stories and putts until either all the beer has been consumed or the pros have gone hoarse from shouting "Way to go!" whenever one of their "Ams" manages to hit something resembling a golf shot. In the hierarchy of Pro-Am partners, Raymond Floyd is a "catch," one of those marquee competitors every amateur dreams of playing with. PGA champion, Masters champion, U.S. Open champion; 60-time winner around the world; Ryder Cup Captain—he almost makes a cliché like "living legend" sound reasonable and appropriate.

One of the world's greatest golf hustlers, a man who has gambled on the links with some of the biggest names in the sport, told me once that the last guy he would want to face in match play would be Ray Floyd. "The man is a trained killer," the hustler explained. And he meant that as a lavish compliment.

During our round at the Dominion, I get to see the hit man up close, working the fairways and greens as though they're so many despotic dictators getting efficiently assassinated. His swing, a jerky backstroke followed by a quick-spinning slash, is not pretty. His putting routine, which includes marching in place to find perfect balance, recalls a barefoot tourist on the hot sands of Acapulco. And his countenance, highlighted by notoriously icy eyes, seems better conceived for a high-stakes poker player or a 10-handicapper who never quite gets the funny old game

just right. You think, *This? This is the stuff of sports history?*
And then you notice that the unlovely swing is the identical efficient motion every time, that the idiosyncratic putting routine usually ends with the ball taking a six-inch
plunge into darkness, that the heartless stare is actually a
hallmark of great heart.

This man can *play*.

In 1993, Tom Watson, captain of the Ryder Cup team,
plucked Raymond Floyd from the Senior Tour, making him
the oldest player ever to compete for his country. Watson
said he was looking for "heart and guts."

Raymond Floyd is heart and guts.

During our round at the Dominion, Floyd and I are ac-
companied by the owner of the golf course, the owner's
banker, and a fellow who used to own one of America's
largest telephone companies. Using the parlance of the business world, you would call this trio "heavy hitters." In any
other parlance, however, you would call them "awestruck
little boys." And you can include me in that unabashed
group. Playing a round of golf with Raymond, you must
constantly suppress the urge to crow, *You da man!* Because
he *is* the man. After watching him drain several testy eight-
footers—our team is getting something like 58 handicap
strokes, and old Raymond is carrying us around the course
like excess baggage—I've got to ask him, "Why does everyone say you're the one guy they would like putting for
them if their life depended on it?"

"Probably because they've seen me do it a few times,"
Raymond Floyd tells me, a mischievous smile curling at
the corners of his mouth. "Back in my day, ball-striking was
a big ego thing. Still is, I guess. But back when everyone
else was beating balls, I figured it was the number you shot
that really mattered. So I started working on my short game
as a kid."

Dave Pelz, the short-game guru, says if you want a role
model for play around the green, the best in the business is
Ray Floyd. Think about it. How many times have you seen
Raymond get up-and-down from oblivion? How many times

have you seen him chip his ball stone dead? How many times have you seen him flush a 12-footer down the drain?

Money player.

Our Pro-Am team doesn't even threaten the top 10. But Raymond, I notice as we pass one of the electronic leaderboards on the back nine, is tied for first. He nods; he grins. He doesn't, however, really care if he wins. "I just want you fellows to have a good time," he says, displaying the smooth charm that has endeared him to legions of corporate sponsors.

This kind of spirit is what's known as "giving something back to the game," a concept frequently talked about, but less frequently executed. Ray Floyd means it. "I love what I'm doing. I love the competition. I love the game. I miss it when I'm away. But my goal is not to be the leading money winner on this Tour. I want to feel competitive. I want an opportunity to win. But this stage of my golf career is really about giving something back."

He says he's seen what an Arnold Palmer appearance can do for a tournament, and he hopes that, "Down the road, my token appearance, my just showing up, might help an event."

I tell him that it's hard to imagine Raymond Floyd making a token appearance. Raymond Floyd never struck me as a man who plays to merely play. Raymond Floyd plays to win.

"That's true. In every event I enter, my goal is to win," he replies. "But at this stage I'm looking for balance in my life. Golf-course design, my business interests, my family. And when the time comes that I can no longer compete, I'll handle that without any problem." He laughs. "I've had a long time to prepare for it!"

Know thyself. It's one of the profound lessons that golf teaches. In Floyd's case, it means employing the same hard focus to his golf career that he does to a double-breaking birdie putt. "I won't play but two events on the regular Tour these days. Doral and the Masters. There are too many guys coming up with a burning desire to win, guys who are willing to make that their number-one priority. I don't *believe* I can win a regular Tour event. Even when I was in contention at Doral this year, I didn't truly believe I could win. Play well, yes. But win? No. Too many young kids who are too strong and who want to be the best."

From such an intense competitor, a man who has had exactly *one* year in his 35-year professional career without a top-five finish, this sounds like sacrilege. Could fierce Raymond Floyd actually be turning mellow? "I'm very happy with what I've done in golf," he says modestly. "I do not desire total devotion. Hard practice for me is forty-five minutes. When I was young, it might have been four hours. These days I practice enough not to embarrass myself." He nods to emphasize his point. "I'm going to enjoy the later stages of my life, enjoy all the things I missed when I was grinding, trying to make something of myself."

❖ ❖ ❖

After our round, in a private corner of the Dominion's stately locker room, Floyd shares a childhood memory, a little secret that, in no small part, reveals why he has become one of the game's all-timers. "I used to compete against myself. Ten balls. I had to get the tenth shot closer to the hole than the previous nine. And I'd say things to myself like, 'If you make this putt, you win the Masters.' I knew if I was going to be any good, I was going to have some of those moments. And when I had them, I wanted to be ready. I wanted to *enjoy* the moment. Then when they came along, later in life, I thought back to all the times I was a kid, and I thought, 'Here you are. This is what you always wanted. And you know what to do.'"

You and I will never know what that's like. (All members of the PGA Tour may disregard the previous sentence.) So I ask Ray Floyd what it *is* like, standing over a putt to win the Masters?

"It's a physical and mental rush," he says. "Electric. But here's the funny part. I go through the same routine, the same thoughts, on a ten-cent putt like I would on a three hundred thousand dollar putt."

There's a lesson for all us hackers. The reason Raymond Floyd can win millions of dollars in five consecutive Senior Skins games against Jack and Arnie and Hale, the reason he's won multiple tournaments in the last four decades, the reason he's the only man in history to win on both the PGA Tour and the Senior Tour in the same year is magical in its simplicity: To Raymond Floyd, $300,000 putts look like 10-cent putts.

Being a money player, it seems, means not worrying about the money.

No, in Floyd's case it means worrying about what really matters. Like his wife, Maria, who he says deserves equal recognition for his success. And his boys, who look to Dad as a role model both on and off the course.

Indeed, when both his sons, Robert and Ray Jr., decided to become professional golfers, Raymond Floyd gave them a short speech. "I told them how difficult their choice might be. 'Boys,' I said, 'there's a lot of downside trying to follow in the footsteps of a famous father. It's a tough and sometimes unfair thing. But I'm thrilled for you. I back you one hundred percent.'"

And then Ray Floyd said, "I have no goals for you. If I can instill one idea, please remember: It's a game. Play for fun. Enjoy the walk. Enjoy the surroundings. Even when it's your job."

10

THE ART
OF THE DRIVE

"Oh, to be long!"
—*Golfer's lament heard in clubhouses throughout America and probably inscribed on an ancient stone somewhere in Scotland.*

John Daly has become one of the most ardently revered golfers in the world for one compelling reason: He hits the ball farther than just about anyone else. We admire him—and are willing to overlook his alcohol-fueled misbehavior and regrettable hair decisions—because he makes a golf ball fly into the great out there the way that all of us who cannot wish we could.

Go ahead and putt for dough. Truth is, virtually any hacker worth his boron-shafted, mega-oversized, titanium-headed instrument of destruction would gladly trade a Crenshaw-like touch on the carpets for the ability to propel a golf ball into another time zone. Oh, to be long. To be preposterously long.

Think about it. What gives you the biggest thrill? Extricating yourself from a buried lie in a deep bunker, setting up a chance to save par? Placing a smoothly struck 2-iron safely in the middle of the fairway, wisely employing mature "course management"? Or blasting a driver so far that the ball virtually disappears from sight, leaving your playing partners agape with envy, murmuring things like "You *crushed* that one" and "That is *large*" and the minimalist but poetically evocative "*Smoke!*"

No wonder, then, that Art Sellinger has carved out a popular and lucrative niche in the world of golf. For years he has delighted thousands of awestruck duffers with exhibitions of his skills, which include driving a golf ball through a telephone book, driving a golf ball 250 yards with a putter, and driving a golf ball 225 yards—while it is still in its sleeve, inside the pro shop's cardboard box packaging.

A few years ago, I saw Art Sellinger and John Daly giving a driving demonstration at a Pro-Am event. After playing a game of tic-tac-toe on a chunk of plywood (they drove golf balls through it to mark their squares), Sellinger and Daly got down to the serious business of driving for show. At the time, Art had a prototype of the now-famous Taylor Made bubbleshaft, which, the theory goes, helps increase clubhead speed, which, the fact is, increases distance. Though I cannot tell you exact yardage—it's hard to see little white orbs more than 300 yards away—if Art and John were playing a match, John often would have been first to hit.

Sellinger, 34, is a two-time North American Long Drive champion and has been the leading money winner in power golf for more than a decade. He does color commentary on The Long Drive contest for ESPN and plays in it too, though someday winning an unprecedented third title, he admits, will be nearly impossible. "Too much preparation and practice required, too little time to get ready," Sellinger says.

Which means that while the winners drive their balls somewhere in the neighborhood of 365 yards, Sellinger's come to rest closer to 350.

That's still forever in my book.

Not long ago I met Art Sellinger at the new Dallas/Fort Worth Tour 18 golf course, near Art's home. Tucked into a gorgeous plot of horse country, the Tour 18 layout, like the wildly popular one in Houston, simulates America's great-

72

est holes. Using aerial photography and computer modeling, designers create vivid reproductions of the originals, such as the "Island Hole" from the TPC at Sawgrass and "Amen Corner" trio from Augusta National. Most hackers will never get to play Pine Valley or Muirfield Village or, for that matter, Augusta. At Tour 18 you can play a hole from all of them.

The golfing public has responded enthusiastically to Tour 18's greatest-hits concept, logging over 60,000 rounds a year at the Houston venue. "We're the golfing capital of corporate America," management crows. New Tour 18s are planned for Las Vegas, Orlando, Atlanta, and San Diego, and construction has begun on the first international branch in Malaysia. Most golfers, it seems, want to be able to say they made bogey on the holes—or nearly identical replicas—they see on television every weekend.

One of the Tour 18 former owners, Barron "7-Iron" Jacobson, invited Sellinger to inaugurate the Dallas/Fort Worth course with him, a bunch of his cronies, and me. Sellinger had the honor of hitting the first official drive off Tour 18's first tee, Cherry Hills #1, where Arnold Palmer, with a now legendary wallop, drove the green en route to winning the U.S. Open. The two-time long-drive champ, who carries four different drivers in an array of lofts and shafts, selected his normal seven-degree club and launched one down the slope toward an emerald target waiting at the bottom. His ball stopped about 30 yards short of the green.

"I guess I'm warmed up now," Sellinger joked.

After the rest of us hit our puny tee shots into a variety of hazards, Art pulled out his big stick, a 48-inch driver. With an explosive, almost violent, crack, he sent a screamer to the right of the green. As the ball reached its apex, it began to draw gently back toward the target, floating as if on a current of hot air, never wanting to come down. Finally, the ball nestled greenside, pin-high.

Cherry Hills #1, you may recall, is a par-4. A 401-yard par-4.

As we played #8 from Baltusrol, another great U.S. Open course, I asked Art what his secret was. "It's not one thing," he explained. "It's a whole bunch of factors coming together at the same time. Basically, you want to get yourself in the best position possible to deliver the blow. And you've got to have clubhead speed." The average Tour pro strikes his drives at 110 miles per hour. Long drivers like Sellinger accelerate the clubhead to 160.

Could he turn me into a big hitter in a few hours? In a word, no. But both Art and Jeff Sheehan, Tour 18's director of golf, did suggest I strengthen my right-hand grip to promote more right-to-left action and add more distance to my shots. The effect was immediate, if inconsistent.

Playing with Sellinger makes you do things you know you shouldn't—like trying to get your ball within 75 yards of his off the tee. The natural tendency for a middle-handicapper like 7-iron Jacobson or me is to swing as fast as Art does. The difference is, he stays in perfect balance; we don't. The results, I'm afraid, speak for themselves.

The disparity between Sellinger's length and the average golfer's can be described as stupendous or depressing, depending on how much you're playing for. On Medinah #10, a 582-yard par-5, Jacobson and I were quite pleased to be within chipping and putting range after hitting driver/fairway-wood/8-iron. Sellinger was putting for eagle after hitting driver/2-iron. At the 425-yard uphill Oakmont #3, with the famous 100-yard "church-pews" bunker, Art hit driver/sand wedge. At Winged Foot #10, a 195-yard par-3, Art hit a 7-iron above the pin. He was 2-under going into Amen Corner.

Tour 18's 14th hole, Firestone #16, is a 625-yard par-5. In competition, the green has been reached in two shots one time each by fellows named Nicklaus, Daly, and Woods. "Here's your chance to make history," Jacobson told Sellinger. "This is the moment we've all been waiting for."

Art stood on the tee box. "Sorry, guys. Not today. The prevailing wind is right in my face. Invite me back here during the winter, when the wind turns around, and I'll get there easy."

Like children at a magic show, we pleaded with Sellinger to at least give it a try, if only for grins. To humor his short-hitting buddies, Art made a gallant effort, hitting his typical 220-feet-per-second scorcher and a monumental 3-wood short of the green-guarding lake. He was left with about 130 yards.

A little three-quarters sand wedge.

11

SELLING SHORT

For a few fleeting moments in my brief golf "career"—
if anything so dismal can be called that—I thought I might
possibly be the best putter in the world. These rare occasions arose because I had somehow managed to make, say,
four putts in a row. ("Hello, Tom Watson? You don't know
me, but I think I can help you with those yips you've been
battling. I'm telling you, I can putt!")

At other, far more frequent, times in my golf career, I
dreaded reaching the green because I knew, I was utterly
certain, that I would suffer yet another humiliating 3-putt.
And, of course, I almost always did. Sometimes a confluence
of spike marks and random luck conspired to miraculously
coax the ball into the cup, but that was only the Cruel Game
mocking my piteous abilities. ("Hello, honey? It's me, at
the clubhouse. Darling, would you remind me why I
thought I could ever play golf?")

I trust you've been there, too, in the ecstatic peaks and
morbid valleys that make golf the most emotionally wrench-
ing sport of them all.

I trust you've mastered the vagaries of ball-striking and,
nevertheless, found yourself incapable of scoring, of cash-
ing in those soaring drives and precise approach shots. I
trust you, like every other person who has played the game,

has muffed, Constantino Rocca-like, a simple little chip. I trust you've hit your 30-yard pitch shots 50 yards and your 50-yarders 20. I trust you have, at particularly depressing moments, taken three to get out of the sand.

If so, it's safe to assume that you have not attended the Dave Pelz Short Game School.

A former physics major at Indiana University with 14 years' experience as a NASA research scientist, Dave Pelz is to golf's short game what Wal-Mart is to retailing. To the dozens of PGA and LPGA touring professionals he counsels, including Curtis Strange, Tom Kite, and Beth Daniel, Pelz is known as "Professor Putt," a tireless scholar who has compiled an extensive body of research on the mysteries of 60-yards-and-in. To the average player, who hears Pelz's name dropped frequently on network golf telecasts— "Ever since Peter Jacobsen saw Dave Pelz during the off-season, he's enjoyed the best year of his career"—he's a mystical oracle with a cult-like following. Indeed, in most of the golf magazines, the phrase "short-game guru" precedes the name "Dave Pelz" with alarming frequency. (Before I saw a photo of him, I envisioned a bearded old man in a turban sitting in the lotus position on Tour practice ranges.) Cult or no, Dave Pelz is generally acknowledged as the world's leading expert on the "scoring game."

That is why I, along with about 20 other hackers of various abilities, recently attended a Dave Pelz Short Game School one-day clinic at the Pelican Hill Golf Club, a beautiful daily-fee complex on California's Newport Coast. The classic three-day school, with Pelz himself in attendance, costs as much as $3,295. The one-day Short Game School "Tour" session, conducted around America by Pelz's assistants, costs $300. The three-hour morning session covers chipping, pitching, and sand play. The three-hour afternoon session covers putting. The entire day is designed to raise confidence and lower scores.

I won't keep you in suspense: It works.

After an intensive day of Dave, I'm back into my "best-putter-in-the-world" mode, and, in my more insane moments, I'm now, again, entertaining fantasies of actually winning the Dave Pelz World Putting Championship.

At the risk of giving away the store, this is what you learn at a Dave Pelz Short Game School. There are no secrets to a successful short game, only good fundamentals. Good ball position, good alignment, good weight distribution—learn these basics and you give yourself a chance to hit it close. To that end, our instructors, led by Dick Wilson, a former Senior PGA player and longtime Pelz acolyte, walk me and my eager colleagues—mostly men in their early 40s bearing the desperate visage of those who have tried every golf tip extant to no avail—through the mysteries of getting up and down.

How important are these skills? Look, for example, at the winners of the four majors in 1995. Only PGA Champion Steve Elkington (28th) was ranked among the top 30 in greens hit in regulation on the PGA Tour. Masters Champion Ben Crenshaw was 159th; U.S. Open Champion Corey Pavin was 100th; and the wild thing, John Daly, the British Open champ, was a dismal 185th. In the same category, the top five money winners fared just as poorly. Greg Norman was 82nd; Billy Mayfair finished 93rd; and Pelz student Lee Janzen was tied with Pavin for 100th. Of the top-10 money winners, only one, Mark O'Meara, was in the top 10 in greens hit. Of the top 40, only three hit many putting surfaces. Instead, they pulled off the finesse shots. They relied on their keen touch around the greens. They *scrambled*. Clearly, the art of pitching, chipping, and putting is what earns the cash.

Dave Pelz stresses that 65 percent of all your golf shots occur within 60 yards of the pin. But most of us spend about 10 percent of our practice time developing this integral facet of our game. (We'd rather be smashing range balls with our new titanium driver.) Why do most amateurs shy away from the short game? Because they're not quite sure *how* to practice. The Dave Pelz Short Game School obviates that uncertainty.

As I discovered at the Pelican Hill clinic, Pelz is big on

training aids, most of which he's personally developed. There's the "bunker board," which trains you to hit effortless sand shots; the "truth board," a perfectly level putting surface that removes all doubt as to the nature of your putting woes; and "the teacher," a nefarious clip attached to your putter, which sends imperfectly struck putts hooking and slicing in all directions like the worst of shanks. Even in six brief hours, Pelz's tools made me better.

I've endured clinics that destroyed what meager shred of game I ever possessed, leaving me dizzy with swing thoughts and mechanical adjustments and ephemeral buzzwords. I departed Pelz's school, however, feeling invincible. I actually hoped that the next time I visited the links, I would *miss* every green.

Thanks to an erratic iron game, when I played both dramatic oceanside layouts at Pelican Hills the next day, I nearly got my wish. And, as my instructors had predicted, I felt marvelously ready for whatever up-and-down challenge lay before me. It's been said that golf is primarily a mental game. If that's so, you have an enormous advantage when you feel prepared and smart and terribly knowledgeable about how to handle what seems to others to be a daunting shot. You *know* you're going to do the right thing. You just know.

I'm in a deep greenside bunker on the Pelican Hills Links course. A *very* deep bunker. The kind in which, when you stand in it, your head is below the surface of the green. The flag is about 10 feet from the edge of the bunker, requiring an explosion shot that sends the ball nearly straight up over the lip of the sand trap and onto the putting surface, where it must land gently and roll slowly toward the hole. In short, the kind of shot, pre-Pelz, that I expected to pull off maybe once in 100 attempts. Now, after being exposed to the Answers, I'll be disappointed if I don't leave myself a reasonable putt for par.

I dig into the sand. I silently review my ball-position checklist; I open the face of my club so it looks as though I'm swinging a spatula; I execute.

I cannot see the ball as it exits the bunker, but when I hear my playing partners shouting, "Go in! Go in the hole!" I know that from now on I won't feel at all silly using the phrase "short-game guru" when I utter the name Dave Pelz.

12

THE MAN WITH
THE GOLDEN SWING

A golf-professional friend of mine has a screen-saver on his personal computer that shows a man in silhouette executing the "perfect" golf swing. By pressing certain buttons on his computer keypad, my friend can make the little shadow-man swing in slow-motion or stop-action from a variety of perspectives. No matter how you look at it, the swing is magnificent.

"The golf swing we're looking at," he tells me, "is supposedly created by taking the best two hundred elements from all the great swings ever captured on film and filtering them through some sort of complex program until you get this, the final product. The ultimate. The perfect swing."

"Sounds complicated," I say.

"Incredibly," he says, studying the shadow man. "Of course, a lot of people don't believe the people who made this screen-saver really went to all that trouble."

"No?"

"Nah. They just copied Steve Elkington."

❖ ❖ ❖

To students of that idiosyncratic enigma called the golf swing, Steve Elkington's version is an *objet d'art*, beauty distilled into steel and leather and combed cotton. If a golf swing were music, Elkington's would be a simple Chopin nocturne, so pretty and ethereal and unbounded by the constraints of mortal effortfulness that it hurts.

"People have always liked my swing," Elkington tells me, speaking with a hybrid accent that suggests his homeland of Australia and his current hometown of Houston. "Even when I was a junior golfer. My swing hasn't always been classical or pretty, but it's been efficient."

Elkington is playing a practice round at Valhalla Golf Club in Louisville, Kentucky, where he'll defend his title at the 78th PGA Championship. While I am tempted to belabor the matter by making strained analogies between certain touring professionals and the Norse Gods—3-woods in place of spears and all that—in deference to the utter simplicity of Steve Elkington's golf swing, I'll merely say this: It is lovely to look at.

And immeasurably more fun than *Gotterdamerrung*.

"I'm always working on rhythm, balance, the fundamentals—like aim and foot position and grip," he says, smoking a 6-iron with inimitable grace. "You get your rhythm and balance down and it tends to look good." When you're walking the fairways with him, close enough to see the dimples on his golf ball, "good" does not adequately describe the looks of his swing. Spend a day with him on the links and you begin to fully appreciate what an impossible task Elkington accomplishes almost every time he puts a club in his hands: He makes the perverse, cruel, wickedly difficult game of golf look easy.

"You just don't seem to *try*," I say, echoing a phrase Elk has probably heard several thousand times since he won the 1995 PGA at Riviera with a stellar final-round 64 and a sudden-death-playoff birdie.

"Oh, I'm trying," he says, smiling. "I like things organized. I like a clean house, everything in its place. Same thing with my golf swing."

Despite possessing broad and powerful shoulders, a cool temperament, and that deliciously elegant swing, Steve

Elkington hasn't walked a finely manicured path strewn with gimme birdie putts. All the pros will tell you a pretty golf swing does not a winner make. (Nor is prettiness a prerequisite for success. Ask Corey Pavin.) Even with his obvious gifts, Elkington claims that when he first joined the Tour in 1987, "I never even thought I would win a tournament. It took me two or three years just to settle down and play my game. To be a major championship winner was certainly something that I only dreamed of as a child, and something I thought I never would experience."

Given his medical affliction, it's a wonder he can even play. Though it sounds like an ailment cooked up by a television comedy writer on urgent deadline, Steve Elkington, professional golfer, is allergic to grass. Which is like being a shortstop allergic to dirt or a basketball player allergic to hardwood floors and shoe contracts. Elk takes antihistamines twice a day and injections twice a week; still, by the end of most rounds he gets a bit red-faced and wheezy. Like an inveterate Puccini lover who's been tricked into sitting through the Ring Cycle—even if it does end at Valhalla and the PGA Championship.

Compounding his travails, Elkington has also had his clubs stolen out of his car—the same clubs he used to win a PGA Tour event five of the first six years of the '90s (an accomplishment matched only by Messrs. Couples, Crenshaw, Love, and Norman), to make the cut in all of the 23 events he entered in 1993, and to capture his first major championship. And not long ago, Elkington weathered his first storm of controversy, a word you normally don't associate with a man generally regarded as among the nicest in the game. (Indeed, during his Valhalla practice round, Elkington dispenses nearly constant instruction to his amateur playing partners, never once displaying a hint of frustration or scorn for their merely human golf swings.) Elk did not compete in this year's Houston Open, his "home" event; instead, he played in Thailand, where a reported six-figure appearance fee was there to greet him.

"Winning anywhere is good," he tells me. "But winning a major gives you worldwide recognition. When I play in Asia, the other professionals stare at me. They just want to *see* the guy who won a major. Some of them literally just want to touch your arm. This last year I've felt like Palmer."

Can you blame him for wanting to get paid like that?

What's happened to Elkington proves that having a pretty swing is nice; being able to win a PGA Championship with it is even better. Some journalists called his closing 64 one of the top 10 rounds of 1995. Elkington thinks that's ridiculous. "My sixty-four wasn't in the top ten of last year," he jokes. "It was in the top ten of all time!"

It may, in fact, take a few more all-timers to win at Valhalla, one of the prettiest—and best-conditioned—golf courses you'll see anywhere. These days the PGA Championship is usually conducted on classic tracks that generate some of the most exciting finishes of the year, for example, Daly out of nowhere at Crooked Stick, Azinger outdueling Norman in extra innings at Inverness, and Elkington making three at the 73rd hole at Riviera. It's also a tournament that doesn't necessarily treat the defending titleholder as a returning hero. I remind Elkington that it's been nearly 50 years since someone (Denny Chute, in 1936 and 1937) won back-to-back PGAs.

"Time to change that," he says with a chuckle. "It's hard to win a major championship. Damned hard. I felt like I maxed out last year, physically and mentally—everything—to do what I did. And," he adds, smiling, "it's a nice feeling, something that no one can take away." But Elkington admits he can't approach the PGA Championship as Just Another Tournament. "Obviously I'm centering my whole year around this tournament. It'll be a big effort for me to come in here and try to be relaxed and play normal because of all the hype. But it's a nice worry to have."

Valhalla may be one of Jack Nicklaus' best designs. It's not a golf course that favors long-ballers. Nor is it necessarily a fairways-and-greens two-putts-and-walk-away kind of short-hitter's course. The fairways are wide off the tee and most of the greens, though surrounded by bunkers, have openings and necks that permit creative approaches. The putting surfaces, come tournament time, may prove severe. So where does all this leave Steve Elkington?

"It's a stern test, a lovely golf course—big driving areas, testing greens on a big major championship kind of site, without any homes surrounding the course. Just meadow on the front side and trees on the back. The bluegrass rough will be a factor. There's a host of people who could do well here," Elkington comments. "A guy like Nick Price is a natural for this tournament. Greg Norman. Phil Mickelson, obviously, would do well, because he putts so well and has a good imagination around these greens."

Elkington smiles, as though he knows a secret that none of the golf journalists or touring professionals or millions of hackers digging up sod at their local goat pasture know. "The guy who hits the most greens in regulation will probably be in the top five here, I would think," he predicts. "The player that wins here will have to hit his irons probably better than anyone else."

In 1996 that man turned out to be Mark Brooks. But watch Steve Elkington swing a 6-iron. Or a 4-iron. Or even the dreaded 1-iron. Watch the man with the golden swing, the one that only a computer can imitate. And then try to bet against him.

13

LONG LAURA

Laura Davies is standing over a 20-foot putt on the seventh green of the New Course at Grand Cypress, the swankiest resort in Orlando. Already this day, several admiring fans have beseeched Laura for an autograph or a posed snapshot, and she has courteously obliged. Now, as she sizes up the break of the green, perhaps daydreaming of the impending day when she can go home to England, put her faithful Maruman clubs in the garage, and be left alone for a few weeks, the next in a nearly continuous stream of admirers comes marching toward her, his hand extended in greeting.

"Laura! Hi," he says, striding boldly onto the putting surface. "I just wanted to stop by and introduce myself. I'm a big fan." The intruding golfer flashes a sheepish grin, the kind usually seen when anonymous hackers confront the power of celebrity face to face.

"Oh, hi," Laura says, her face breaking into a wide smile.

"Corey Pavin. Really pleased to meet you."

For a few minutes I stand sandwiched between Laura Davies and Corey Pavin as they chat, willing my body to absorb a fraction of their collective golf greatness, if only through some sort of para-normal osmosis. They talk of upcoming schedules and tournaments they've recently played—typical professional golfer stuff—and I wonder if

Laura is thinking, "I wish I had this guy's short game." As someone who hits it about as far as Corey Pavin does off the tee, I *know* what he's thinking: "Tiger, shmiger. There's no telling how many tournaments I might win if only I had this lady's length."

Yes, the prodigious distance Laura Davies can propel a golf ball is coveted by nearly everyone who plays the game. One who doesn't is John Daly—who annually selects Laura to be his partner in the end-of-the-year, mixed-team, JC Penney event.

Indeed, this day, a few days after Laura spent a week playing with Long John, she's attacking the Grand Cypress layout with a golf ball adorned with an Arkansas Razorback, a gift from the Wild Thing. In many ways, she and Daly are kindred spirits: They both hit the ball frightfully far; they both play fast (when they're paired behind a plodding couple like Tiger Woods and Kelli Kuehne, it's like dying a slow death); and they both live life to the hilt—and sometimes beyond.

But on the matter of their results, that's where the similarities end. Daly is constantly struggling to put together four decent rounds. Davies' struggle is grander: to win every tournament she enters.

In 1996, another magnificent season for the number-one female player in the world, Laura Davies won the European money title and narrowly missed doing the same on the American tour, finishing second to Karrie Webb. The 1997, '98, and '99 campaigns, however, were less brilliant. Laura lost her top ranking and slid down the money list while players like Juli Inkster and Annika Sorenstam tried (vainly) to curtail Webb's dominance.

Laura Davies is well-acquainted with the vicissitudes of the game. She's been punishing golf balls since the age of 14 when, for no particular reason, she picked up one of her brother's golf clubs and started swinging. Like the pre-school genius who sits down at the piano and starts playing Mozart by ear, young Laura discovered almost immediately that she had a gift for ball-striking. She was a prodigy, a teenage girl who could hit it as far—or farther—than the boys. "I've always been able to hit the ball," she says. "Right from the start I could hit it a long way. Playing with my brother and the other boys, I'd be ridiculed if I didn't."

Her talent grew steadily, but not because an influential mentor guided her junior career. "I've never had a lesson in my life," one of the world's best female golfers says. "Not one. Never wanted one. I always thought the best way to get better was to figure things out myself." To this day, "swing doctors" on the prowl at LPGA practice ranges know to stay away from her; she doesn't want their advice. "They'd just muck things up," Davies says.

Some cynics have suggested that the present-day Laura would do well to get a check-up. Her swing is anything but classical—a Palmeresque slash from the top of her downswing; up on the toes at impact; crater-like divots in its wake—but, like most effective golf swings, it mirrors the personality of the swinger. It's not pretty; it's imposing; and even under immense pressure, it usually works. This is a golfer who has often relied on her extraordinary power to beat a golf course. Where others are hitting 5-irons into greens, she's hitting a 9-iron. When others are playing from the fairway 175 yards from the hole, she's often playing from the rough—but only 130 yards from the pin. Since Laura Davies is accustomed to bombing flags from manageable distances, she's never had a particularly potent short game, and her putting has been, at best, average.

Laura Davies is held to higher standards than most lady golfers because, for many years, she has played in a separate, slightly elevated realm than the rest of her colleagues. It has almost always been this way for her.

After a productive amateur career—she left school at 16 to concentrate on golf—Davies turned pro at 21 and quickly began her ascent to the pinnacle of her profession. In 1986 she won the British Open. To date, she's won more than 60 tournaments world-wide. How good is she? More than a few PGA pros believe Laura Davies could earn a fine living on *their* tour.

91

When we meet in Florida to play a round of golf, I instinctively address her as "Ms. Davies."

She says, "That's rather formal, isn't it?"

I tell her I want to speak respectfully to a proper English lady, the kind who says "cheers" when you concede a tap-in par putt. She laughs and says, "I'm a proper English lady, but I'm not formal. And sometimes I'm not even proper!"

Whether some of Laura Davies' habits are proper or not is a matter best adjudicated by the arbiters of etiquette, a task for which I am woefully unqualified. All I know is that Laura Davies is fun. Her grip-it-and-rip-it golf game is fun. Her bonhomie is fun. Watching her exploits around the world, you get the sense that she would be the kind of person with whom you'd like to share a beer—a warm and dark one, preferably—after a care-free round on the links. This is a woman who owns a red Ferrari 456 that goes something like 189 mph. She takes it to Germany once a year just to drive it the way it's meant to be driven.

When we get in our golf cart, she says politely but firmly, "I'll drive." I don't argue.

Another of Laura's passions, widely reported in the golf and sports press, is America's unofficial favorite pastime: gambling. For her, constantly traveling and constantly competing, high-stakes gambling provides a much-needed respite. "It's strictly entertainment," she tells me—if you can call wins and losses said to be in the six figures entertaining. I ask her if she fancies any particular game. Blackjack? Craps? Golf? "I like them all," Davies says.

Knowing this, I propose that we play for a little something, "little" being the operative word. "Sure, whatever you'd like," she says.

We settle on a friendly $10 Nassau ($10 for the front nine; $10 for the back nine; $10 overall) with one crucial condition: Manhood and pride be damned, she has to spot me five strokes a side. "Whatever you'd like," Laura says, generously.

From the onset of our match, I can tell that Davies has

not brought her best game to Grand Cypress. A vexing toothache—exacerbated by windy conditions—and a balky putter conspire to prevent her usual barrage of birdies. If she were one of my buddies, one of the hooligans I normally play with back home, I would probably have the needle out and ready for frequent and well-timed insertions. (As would my buddies for me, bless their larcenous hearts.) But this isn't a duffer I'm tangling with; it's Laura Davies. *Laura Davies.* I feel like I should be asking her permission to joke.

Ms. All-in-Good-Fun, that's her. Laura Davies is the kind of marvelously well-adjusted superstar who makes a sod-digging amateur feel as though he can get away with an affectionate barb—and that she might even enjoy it.

For the entire round I encourage her (not very subtly) to perhaps consider hitting something other than her Maruman driver off the tee. A 2-iron, maybe. This is not because I'm concerned about her course management; it's because I am praying for the moment when I might actually hit my tee ball past hers. I figure it's not often a guy gets the chance to say to Laura Davies, "So, does your husband play golf?"

Alas, with the exception of one lay-up hole that has a creek in the landing area, it's an afternoon of Driving Miss Davies.

Despite the ignominy of always hitting my second shot first—"You're away!" Laura sweetly reminds me—I find a few opportunities for less than Shakespearean ripostes. When she leaves a long birdie putt well short and I chirp, "You might want to wipe the mascara off that putter," Davies laughs heartily—and promptly rams home a 12-footer. "Oh, no!" I cry in mock horror. "I got her mad."

At this she laughs even louder.

And why shouldn't she? She's used to battling the likes of Webb and Sorenstam and Pepper every week. The prospect of losing $30 to a cackling idiot who has to beg for five strokes per side bothers Laura Davies about as much as breaking a tee. She has a six-acre garden at her villa outside of London, near Wentworth, awaiting her. And a tennis court. And a football pitch. Both of which she uses with great vigor when she's home, which is almost never.

Laura Davies doesn't need much, except to have a good time.

She is the kind of easy-going, fun-loving, regular gal with whom you immediately feel at ease. (The only thing intimidating about Davies is her overwhelming golf game, which can make even the most sober observer giggle in awe.) Not many other major championship winners would make you feel well within your rights to say, when standing over a three-foot putt you're hoping they'll concede, "Need a tetanus shot, Laura? Got a bad case of lockjaw?"

Beneath her good nature, though, I sense a weariness in Laura Davies, the cost, I assume, of interminably racing around the world, testing her talent and will nearly every week of the year. It is the price she pays for attempting to be the greatest.

Have you ever wondered what it must be like to be the best in the world at something? At anything? What it must be like to know that of all the people walking this planet you—and only you—are the greatest? Laura Davies has often traveled the world with that knowledge.

I ask her how important it is to be ranked number-one in the world. "I'd be lying if I said it wasn't very important to me," Davies says, preparing to launch a drive on an inviting par-5. "Every week when I pick up a golf magazine, the first thing I look at is the Ping Leaderboard [the female equivalent of the male Sony Rankings]. I'm very proud to have hung on to number one for over two years now, but, honestly, it was never a goal. I never sat down and thought, 'I want to be the top-ranked golfer in the world.' But once it happened," she smiles warmly, "I've made it a point to keep it. That's my intention."

Davies, since our rendezvous in Florida, has let it slip from her grasp. There's a new breed of champions on the LPGA Tour, and they're more likely to steamroll the competition than be intimidated by it. But just as Tiger Woods has raised the level of excellence in the men's game—you want to win, you've got to play better than Eldrick—the young guns will force established superstars like Davies to find another gear.

I think she will, too. I'm not certain for how long or by how much. But I do know this: Laura Davies will battle mightily to be the greatest female golfer in the world, meeting that rare challenge with the same unfettered ferociousness with which she goes after a golf ball teed high.

And I know this as well: She'll have fun trying.

14

THE CURSE
OF LEFTY

He's got a putting stroke as languid and lovely as the sun setting on the Sonoran Desert.

He's got a short game as imaginative and delightful as a Coen Brothers movie.

He's won over a dozen times on the PGA Tour, more than Sergio Garcia and Colin Montgomerie combined.

He's got a mansion (with a 2,500-foot putting green in the backyard) and a jet (with a pilot's license to fly it) and many millions of dollars in earnings.

He has his own Web site.

He has his health.

He's married to the type of woman *Sports Illustrated* typically features in its swimsuit edition. (In fact, in 1998 they appeared in the magazine as a couple. He wore trunks; she wore a swimsuit brought from home, in lieu of a more provocative number *SI* provided).

He's never not been a winner, starting as a youngster and continuing to the present. There has not been a year in the last 10 that he has not won some kind of golf tournament. Three-time Junior Player of the Year. U.S. Amateur champion. NCAA champion. He won the PGA Tour's Tucson Open as an amateur, while he was still a student at Arizona State, but declined to turn professional. He wanted to earn his degree—and claim another NCAA Player of the Year title. (Three of those, too).

Phil Mickelson has it all. Except for one thing.

As the PGA Tour barrels through the 2000 season, Phil Mickelson does not have a major championship victory.

This, if you happen to pay attention to the game's great pontificators, is a dismal state of affairs bordering on tragedy. Bearing headlines like "Unful-Philled" and "Major Void," preview stories bemoaning Mickelson's unrealized potential appear each year before the Masters, PGA Championship, and U.S. and British Opens as predictably as a Tiger Woods pout. When will he win one? Why hasn't he won one? How can he win one? The standard wisdom is "it's just a matter of time" and "it's not *if* he'll win one, but *how many* he'll win." Eventually, the reasoning goes, the stars will align correctly and Lefty will take his rightful place in the pantheon of golf immortals.

He came within a few excruciating putts of breaking through at Pinehurst in 1999. And it seems obvious that eventually all his near misses will be washed away by victory.

In the meantime, Phil Mickelson is stuck with the inglorious yoke worn previously by Tom Kite, Davis Love III, and Mark O'Meara: The Best Player Never to Have Won a Major.

This dubious honor is largely the creation of the broadcast media, a convenient label that produces instant protagonists when the drama quotient starts to run low during the annual quests for Claret Jugs and green jackets. Still, it weighs on the players. Before he defended his PGA Championship title at Sahalee, Davis Love told me, "The media definitely created the Best Player Never to Have Won a Major thing. But the pressure to win one of these tournaments comes from the *player*. We *want* to win a major. So passing the label on to someone else is a great relief."

And now Phil Mickelson is that guy. (Never mind that in the eyes of many golf observers David Duval is probably the *true* heir to the crown.) Being that guy is a tough burden to bear—especially when you're only 29 years old.

"I'm not that stressed out about it," Phil Mickelson tells

me. "It's a compliment in a way. There are so many guys, so many great players that haven't won a major. To be regarded as one of the best is an honor."

We're walking the fairways of Forest Oaks Country Club in Greensboro, North Carolina, where Phil is in town for the Greater Greensboro Open. I have to keep reminding myself that this seasoned veteran of the PGA Tour, this Ryder Cup member, this *superstar*, is still in his 20s. Phil Mickelson the man is as polished as Phil Mickelson's golf game. Possessing a shy smile that could charm even the most curmudgeonly of misanthropes, he's articulate and polite and thoughtful. And enormously competitive.

"To be honest," he says, "if I only won one tournament a year for the rest of my career, I'd be disappointed." Majors would (will?) be great, but, as Mickelson correctly suggests, there are many tournaments that have fields equivalent to majors. He wants to win those, too.

It's not that the majors don't "set up" well for him. He likes hard courses. He likes firm greens and tough rough. He *likes* golf courses prepared as they are in major championships. "I'm tired of seeing twenty-under win on Tour," Mickelson remarks. "I'd like to see five- or six-under win." He's placed third twice in majors and held the 36-hole lead as recently as the 1998 PGA Championship. Only Payne Stewart's brilliance denied him at Pinehurst #2. He most certainly has got the game to win. And yet ...

"I've come to a realization. I'm going to hit bad shots. Bad chips, bad putts. Shots people don't expect from me. It's part of the game. The perception of me always being great is incorrect," Mickelson explains. "The challenge in a major is not to give in to the pressure. When I'm in contention, my instincts are to attack the pin, to make birdies, to win. I'm learning that in a major your instinct has to be to outlast your opponents."

Mickelson's longtime caddie, Jim "Bones" MacKay, says, "The great asset in Phil's game is that he has about twenty yards in reserve. He'll normally hit his three-wood about two fifty. But he can step it up to two seventy when he needs it." Ironically, it may be stepping *down* that will win Mickelson his spot in history.

❖ ❖ ❖

Phil Mickelson is far too wily to let a writer corner him with a blunt question like, "What are your goals?" He deflects such intrusions with a modest, "My goals are sort of personal." But he does acknowledge goals that have nothing to do with major championships. Goals that have nothing to do with how many times he strikes a golf ball. The really important stuff.

"My most important goal is to treat people fairly," Mickelson reveals. "I work hard on my game. But I work just as hard on how I handle myself. When I come home to my wife at the end of a day, I'm more concerned with 'did I handle myself on and off the golf course as well as I possibly could?' than how I played."

I encourage anyone who cares about golf to reread the previous sentence. In an age when professional athletes mistake their multi-million dollar compensation packages for an unrestricted license to behave like jerks, it's heartening to know that there's at least a few multi-millionaire athletes out there like Phil Mickelson who may still reasonably be considered role models.

In Greensboro, during the Pro-Am, the standard bearer (the person who holds the sign displaying the player's score) for Phil's group is a young man with Down's Syndrome. When Mickelson learns from the lad's father that the boy's favorite golfer happens to be a rangy lefty with the world's prettiest putting stroke, Mickelson, I notice, does not merely shake the young man's hand, like a formality to be dispatched with. He stops what he's doing— visiting with the corporate bigshots in his foursome—and walks up the fairway with the boy, chatting about golf and Greensboro and anything else that might interest his sign-toting new friend. This is not a five-second visit. Or even a 30-second one. It's a leisurely engaging walk. Phil signs an autograph and takes a picture with him and says, "If there's anything else I can do for you, let me know." The boy's father blinks away a tear: He knows his son will never forget this moment.

Mickelson smiles. "It's cool to be in a position to make somebody's day, to make a difference in their life."

According to Bones, Phil signs more autographs than anyone on Tour. "It's a fact," Bones says. "Especially for kids."

I notice that Phil Mickelson has something of a double standard when it comes to autographs. If an adult asks him for a signature, Phil politely says he'd be happy to oblige— as soon as he's done with his round. If a *child* asks, however, Phil will invariably oblige on the spot. "It wasn't that long ago when I was looking up to professional golfers, wishing I could be like them," he explains. "I can relate to juniors. I know making eye contact, saying 'hello'—that goes a long way."

Spending a day with Phil Mickelson, you come to understand that these sentiments are not just easy pronouncements cooked up for him by a stable of handlers. They're his beliefs, sacred sacraments of PGA Tour celebrity. Over lunch in the clubhouse, Mickelson could easily regale me with the usual airy athletic nonsense about "giving one hundred ten percent" and "getting the job done" that fills the morning sports pages. Instead he talks about golf's vaunted "next generation." I'd love for him to compare himself to Ernie and Tiger and Justin—all winners of major championships, incidentally—but Phil, the "old man" of the young crowd, has only this to say:

"We—all of us who will be playing this game for the next ten or twenty years—need to conduct ourselves in a positive way. The former generations, they were total professionals. It's so important for us to treat people right, not taking for granted what we do. We have to appreciate that the fans allow us to play this game for a living. I'm talking about basic people skills. There's a right way to approach the public and a wrong way. We—me, Tiger, all of us—need to make sure we're doing things the right way."

If you care about golf, you can reread that sentence, too.

Phil Mickelson does not have a major championship to his name. But anyone who watches him and doesn't see a major winner should look again.

15

BETTER LATE
THAN NEVER

In case you haven't yet stumbled upon the essential truth about the grand old game of golf, I'll share it with you: Golf—besides being a perfectly poetic little microcosm of life itself—is irony incarnate. Got that? Golf is irony.

For example, swing as hard as you can and produce a pathetic dribble; swing rhythmically and in balance, and *voila!* Practice four hours a day, buy a garage full of swing aids, and watch your handicap balloon by six strokes; then put the sticks away for a few weeks, mount the first tee with nary a warm-up bucket, and shoot your low round of the year.

Ironic, no?

If you remain unconvinced, allow me to introduce you to a fellow named Jim Colbert.

Jim Colbert, old enough to be a member of AARP, could save $8 when he takes his wife Marcia to the movies; Jim Colbert, old enough to be a member of AARP, will not accept the discounted price because, he says, "I am *not* a senior, no way!"

Jim Colbert, an enormously successful 57-year-old athlete, was the Senior PGA Tour's leading money winner two years in a row, earning a then-record $1,627,890 in 1996; Jim Colbert, an enormously successful businessman, does not need the money.

Jim Colbert's biggest liability on the "junior circuit," the PGA Tour, was his body; Jim Colbert's biggest asset on the Senior Tour is his body.

Jim Colbert, a tenacious fiercely competitive champion, is perceived by many who don't know him as an arrogant cocky little cuss; Jim Colbert, a tenacious fiercely competitive champion is, to those who do know him, about the nicest millionaire-superstar-celebrity you'd ever want to work, play, or chat with.

"I guess you could say I share how I'm feeling out on the golf course," Colbert tells me. We're in his hometown, Las Vegas, touring Desert Pines, a new golf course owned by one of Colbert's long-time friends. "I'm an open book. Sometimes people mistake friendliness and sharing your feelings for cockiness."

If you played golf as well as Jim Colbert, you might have reasonable grounds to occasionally behave cockily. Even with the matriculation of young bucks like Hale Irwin to the Senior Tour, Colbert won five times in '96, finished second five times, and cracked the top 25 in 23 of the 32 tournaments he entered. Over the past two years he has won nine times; his next closest competitor, Bob Murphy, has won six times. At the close of the '96 campaign, locked in a ferocious battle for the money title with youthful Mr. Irwin, Colbert had a streak of two wins, two runner-ups, and a third. He clinched the number-one spot at the Tour Championship where, on the 72nd hole at the Dunes Golf & Beach Club in Myrtle Beach, he needed to sink a twisting 12-footer to preserve his role as top dog. If a guy nicknamed Tiger hadn't been having a similar streak of his own at the same time, Colbert's gutsy stellar play would likely have been the golf story of the moment.

The man has clearly earned his bragging rights.

Only there's no braggadocio about him. In Jim Colbert, the physical quirks that some television viewers consider the affectations of unabashed arrogance are, in fact, organic manifestations. The floppy bucket hat, which makes him look like the Gilligan of the Senior circuit, and the jauntily

104

upturned collar are both idiosyncrasies he's had since he was 16, when he fainted from sunstroke while competing in the Kansas City amateur championship. The crooked swaggering walk is, like so much of Jim Colbert's persona, a product of his lifelong back problems: One shoulder tends to ride higher than the other. And as for "the gesture"—the thumb and forefinger extended like a pistol and a crisp snap of the wrist, usually performed after draining a key putt—there's a little-known story behind that.

"I'll tell you where that comes from," Colbert says, admiring the panoramic view of downtown Las Vegas from Desert Pines' 17th tee. "Luther Fisher, he's the guy responsible for this," Colbert tells me, performing his personal victory move. Fisher, it turns out, was an ESPN cameraman. Colbert spent his first year on the Senior Tour after three years of working as an ESPN golf analyst. His former broadcast colleagues, including the guys behind the cameras, were rooting for him. Early in his Senior career, Colbert made a difficult birdie putt to put him in contention to win the tournament. As he walked off the green and the gallery roared its approval, Fisher stepped from behind his camera and made the pistol gesture directly at his old buddy, as if to say, "Yes! You can do it!" Colbert, delighted by the enthusiastic support, responded in kind, "just like I was waving back at him," he says.

What he didn't know was that Fisher's television camera was still "hot," still broadcasting images of him. Among the millions of viewers who witnessed the celebratory moment were all the other ESPN cameramen at the tournament, who subsequently mimicked the gesture when Colbert passed their cameras. "And I did it right back," he remembers. By the time Colbert walked off the 18th green, a trademark had been born.

"After about two years of doing it I started to feel uncomfortable," Colbert admits. "But it had become something people expected of me. Like Chi-Chi's sword dance. I mean, even kids liked it." These days, Colbert says, he often tries to hide the gesture—"I do it sort of subtle, sort of half-

105

hearted"—which is why it sometimes comes off looking smug, just as a repressed smile sometimes appears to be a smirk. Yet fans still love and expect the move. As Colbert and I make our way around Desert Pines, every other golfer driving past in a golf cart affectionately shoots us.

"See what I mean?" he exclaims, laughing.

Jim Colbert is a man who thoroughly enjoys the notoriety he's earned. For his entire professional career on the junior circuit, he was known as a "journeyman," if that can be said of someone who won eight times on the PGA Tour, seven of them official money-event wins. "Winning a whole bunch of tournaments and money titles—I never had that on the junior Tour," Colbert says, surveying the majestic mountains around us. "Money is not the point now. Winning is the point. I'm into competing every week like I was playing for the club championship in the 'C' flight. And you know what? I don't think I'd trade my success now for success back then. Because I appreciate it more. Never having it when I was younger, after so much struggle and pain—believe me, I appreciate everything I've got now."

The pain Colbert refers to is not the psychological kind, the dull ache that afflicts so many hundreds of very good professional golfers who are somehow not quite good enough. Colbert's pain was the physical kind.

"My back was so bad on the junior Tour, after warming up I'd hit my best drive of the day on the first tee," Colbert recalls. "By the time I got to the first green I'd be tight. It was all downhill from there. Sometimes, by the time I'd get to the last tee, I could hardly swing the club."

About three years ago Jim Colbert discovered what for him has become the Holy Grail of spinal health: magnets. "I wear them on my back and neck. They're about the size of coins; you don't even know they're on you." He shows me the career-saving dots. Attached to his skin with adhesive strips, they look like so many nicotine patches. He wears them constantly, travels with a special magnetized mattress, and has a magnetized seat cushion on his Sabreliner 80 jet. "Tectonic magnets," he says, smiling broadly. "I don't hurt anymore. Not in my hands, not in my knees. I'm older than ever and I've never felt better."

The proof, of course, is in his play. "I can hit it farther now than I did five years ago," Colbert reports. "My driving distance has actually *increased* about twelve yards since I began my Senior career. But I've discovered that Senior golf isn't about distance." Shortly before defending his title at the Toshiba Senior Classic in Newport Beach, California, Colbert tells me, "Strength is not the problem if you stay active. Probably fourteen of the top fifteen guys work out very hard. So that's part of it. But our game, a successful Senior golf game, is fifty percent physical and fifty percent mental. If you can't do both, you've got the worst of it."

Colbert, clearly, can do both.

Though he didn't finish in the top five in a single statistical category last year—indeed, he finished in the top 10 three times (ninth in scoring, ninth in birdies, and 10th in putting)—Jim Colbert won the cash. I ask him how this is possible. "I'm not real long; I'm a player. I can get the ball around the course and get it in the hole. And I'm a real good finisher."

His temperament, Colbert says, is what makes him a consistent winner. "I get excited without falling down dead. Playing in a golf tournament is like barely avoiding being hit by a Mack truck. It's that rush of adrenaline and fear. I can get real fear playing golf," Jim Colbert says, not without a palpable sense of irony. "How you handle those nerves makes all the difference. Nerves are neutral. They don't affect you until you direct them. You can either direct them to add stress and tension or you can direct them at the job at hand." He smiles boyishly. "I direct them to the job at hand."

Some Senior stars, Jack Nicklaus among them, have said that the week-in week-out demands of competition wear on them, exacting a psychological toll that, frankly, they're not interested in at this stage in their lives. "Me, it's what I like to do," Colbert says. "I am competitive, I admit it. Between the gallery ropes I'm just pure competitiveness. I'm a trained killer. Now, to some people that word might be synonymous with addictive or driven, which in some other areas of life might not be so great. Even in golf my wife might not think it's so great! But let me tell you: There's nothing I'd rather be doing than playing tournament golf."

His face is burnished with contentment. And for a moment Jim Colbert, 57, looks, ironically, like a care-free boy, a lad with nothing but play on his mind. "Sometimes I ask myself, 'What else would you rather do? Retire?'" Colbert laughs. "I'd just end up sitting around the house. And playing golf."

16

SWEDE DEMON

No matter how evolved a man you are, no matter how liberated and egalitarian and all the other admirable and fancy things you believe yourself to be—when you play golf with Helen Alfredsson, your oversized male ego will crumble like a three-day-old croissant.

It happened to me. And I suspect it would happen to just about any man whose game is not as solid as his political convictions. I *know* Helen Alfredsson is a wildly talented LPGA star; I *know* that when we play she's supposed to trounce my sorry butt; I *know* I should be resigned to the fact that she will play great and I will not. Still ...

Here is the problem with a youngish, competitive, divorced man playing golf with Helen Alfredsson: She is a youngish, competitive, (engaged) woman who, in addition to being tall and beautiful and graceful, is frightfully long. As in much longer than your average golf writer-hacker.

She hits the ball very far. And straight.

When I first meet Helen Alfredsson, in Kissimmee, Florida, where she's helping Taylor Made launch its new line of Bubble Burner irons, I want badly to play well. Too badly, probably. On the first four holes she makes wide, rhythmic, classically powerful swings, in the style of Davis Love III; I hit 140-yard pop-ups off the tee, in the style of a hapless fool. She's not trying; I'm trying too hard. She makes pars; I make double-bogeys. She's doing what she does best, looking good doing it; I'm looking for someplace to hide.

In the course of our round, I discover that Helen and I are neighbors. Her long-time fiancée, Leo Cuellar, a professional soccer player she met while attending the United States International University in San Diego, lives in the Los Angeles area, and when Helen isn't touring with the LPGA, she's often there. "We should play sometime in Los Angeles," she says casually. Imagining showing up at my local club with Helen Alfredsson—"Yo, Mike, who's the babe?"—makes me even more nervous.

Helen Alfredsson, a six-year LPGA veteran, hits the ball the way most amateurs dream of hitting it, typically with a soft right-to-left draw. Her shots are guided missiles. They are very pretty, like her accent and her blue eyes.

Helen Alfredsson is Swedish, and her perfect English has a charming sing-songy character to it. Though some in the (mostly male) golf press have referred to her as a "Swedeheart," her on-course demeanor is anything but warm and cuddly. After imperfect shots, she growls and sometimes utters a brief explosive oath. She frequently talks to her ball—"Get *left!* Come *on!*"—in a tone that does not invite contradiction. And when she sticks one close, she will often allow herself a victorious pump of the fist and a joyous "*Yes!*" Helen Alfredsson does not hide her feelings, on or off the golf course.

So outspoken is she that journalists sometimes wonder if Alfredsson knows she's on the record when she joins them for a round of golf. Of her sponsor, Taylor Made, offering a lucrative contract to the fickle Lee Janzen: "The guy has no loyalty, and he definitely has no credibility. Why would they sign someone like him? I think it looks bad."

Of the disparity in prize money between the men's and women's tours: "It's a man's world we live in; I understand this. I'm just glad to be able to earn a living playing golf, even if it isn't as much as the men on the PGA Tour. That doesn't bother me. What pisses me off is seeing how much the Seniors are making, playing on Mickey Mouse golf courses, shooting twenty-under par."

Of the LPGA's "image" problem: "Isn't it terrible that some of our players are judged by what they look like, and not on what kind of person they are? Would we all be more popular if we wore more makeup?"

Naturally, Alfredsson's candor has made her popular in some quarters and loathed in others. That, she says, does not concern her. "Having an opinion and being able to express it—that's supposed to be one of the great things about America. That's one of the reasons I love living here."

Though her first Tour win was the 1993 Nabisco Dinah Shore, an LPGA "major," most of the world discovered Alfredsson's frank unbowdlerized style in 1994, shortly after she suffered one of the most horrifying collapses in major tournament golf. In the opening round of the U.S. Open at Indianwood Golf & Country Club in Lake Orion, Michigan, Alfredsson posted a record-breaking 63. In her second round, Alfredsson shot a 69, breaking both the men's and women's 36-hole records. Midway through the third round, when she reached an unthinkable 13-under par—this was the U.S. Open, after all, where even par is sometimes good enough to win—Helen Alfredsson was playing the kind of golf that not only wins tournaments but makes history.

And then she fell apart. She lost her game. Literally. "It's very hard to describe what happened to me," she says, surveying a birdie putt at the Wilshire Country Club in Los Angeles. "It wasn't an emotional reaction to the situation, to the pressure. It was a physical thing. I couldn't feel *anything* in my hands," Alfredsson says, wide-eyed. "I couldn't see. Before the middle of Saturday, all I could see were the pins, like radar. Then, all of a sudden, nothing. It was very scary."

Alfredsson played her last 29 holes in 14-over par, placing ninth, eight strokes behind the champion, Patty Sheehan. In the 1993 Open, she had blown a two-stroke lead and finished second. This time it was seven strokes. "Of course I wanted to run away, to sit in a corner and cry. But I made myself go before the cameras," she recalls. After finishing her round Alfredsson spoke openly on national television, explaining to the world what it felt like to fail on such a grand scale. She was composed, honest, and charismatic. Anyone who saw her that painful day had to like her: In a world filled with *prima donna* athletes, this golfer, you could see, was a class act. Here was the rare public figure who, in her darkest moments, inspired not pathos but empathy.

No wonder, then, that her four-stroke victory the next week on Tour meant as much to her as it did to everyone who loves golf. "That next week may have been the most important week of my career," Alfredsson tells me, shortly before unleashing a wickedly long drive on an inviting par-5. "Not only did I have to make myself put aside all the doubts and go back out and play, but I had to deal with having the lead again, with having the opportunity to win. It's one thing to come from behind and not quite get there. It's another thing to be out front. If I would have folded up again, one week after the Open, who knows if I would have ever been the same player. But," she says, smiling, "I'm still here."

When not playing golf, Alfredsson enjoys, among other things, well-made shoes and driving automobiles at high speeds. "Going fast is a good release for my temper, I guess," she explains. Not long ago the 31-year-old golfer attended a professional drag-racing school in Florida with four players from the men's Tour. Alfredsson ran off the fastest quarter-mile time in the group.

Beating the men is not new to her. A big redheaded tomboy, Helen Alfredsson started playing golf when she was 11, in her native Goteborg. By 14 she was the youngest member of the Swedish junior national team. And before she departed for the lucrative challenges of the LPGA and European Tours (where she won the Women's British Open), Alfredsson had captured the Swedish national championship six times.

Why, I ask her, should Sweden, a cold sparsely populated country, produce so many world-class athletes, first in tennis and now in golf? "You don't have to be a child of privilege there," she said. "Sweden has a national sports program that identifies talent early and supports them, no matter what their economic status. In some ways smallness has its advantages."

I tell Helen this sounds funny coming from a nearly six-foot-tall woman who hits her ball farther than most men. "You know what's funny about playing with men, especially the successful wealthy ones I see a lot in our Pro-Ams?"

"They're intimidated by you?" I guess from experience.

"No. They refuse to hit more club than I do. If I hit a seven-iron, they have to hit an eight. If I hit an eight, they hit a nine." She laughs lightly. "Once I'm standing on the tee of a par-three with a famous man, whose name I can't tell you. I hit a five-iron pin high. He asks me, 'What did you hit? Three?' I tell him I hit a five. So he says, 'Well, what do you think I should hit? Six? Seven?' I said to him, 'Hit whatever club you want. You haven't gotten it out of your shadow all day, anyway!'"

Did he appreciate her evaluation, I wonder?

"Oh, we had a good laugh. I think most people appreciate when you're honest with them," Alfredsson says.

Indeed. When I finally hit a decent wedge late in our round together, a *good* shot within 10 feet of the pin, Helen whoops and yells enthusiastically, "Great shot!" Coming from her it feels good. No, let's be honest: It feels great.

17

THE JOCKEY WHO
BECAME A BULLDOG

"I'm a perfectionist. The word *contentment* is not in my vocabulary much."

Who said it: retired General Norman Schwarzkopf, at a motivational speaking engagement; hard-charging CEO Michael Eisner, demanding larger profits at a Disney board meeting; despotic murderer King Richard III, at the beginning of Shakespeare's play about him; or former U.S. Open Champion Corey Pavin, at dinner a few weeks before attempting to win another major golf championship?

Even if you're not a golf fan, you've probably deduced that the fellow in question is too slim to be Schwarzkopf, too mustachioed to be Eisner, and too tan to be King Richard.

Corey Pavin, it is true, is seldom content. Which is not to say he is seldom happy. Corey Pavin, actually, is a very happy person. (Great family, devout faith, mounds of endorsements—what's not to be happy about?) He's just not a complacent person. When you're always striving for perfection—especially in a game that's all about imperfection—there's not much opportunity for complacency.

"Trying to get better at golf is like a dog chasing its tail," he says. "You never quite get there." We're dining at a lovely restaurant overlooking the practice putting green at the Doral Resort and Country Club in Miami, site of the Doral Ryder Open, where many of the PGA Tour's star players begin their campaigns toward golf's four major championships. Jack Nicklaus is two tables away, squeaking out his avant-garde rendition of "Happy Birthday" to his wife Barbara. Ben Crenshaw and Phil Mickelson and Vijay Singh wander past. Peter Kostis waves hello. Tonight there's more golf knowledge and skill congregated in this dining room than in all the country club grills in America. Given the view, I am thankful that the Florida sun is dipping below the horizon, lest Pavin leave me and his lobster bisque in favor of rolling in a few more six-footers.

He's telling me about playing the U.S. Open. "I'm going to approach the Open the way I do every tournament," Pavin says. "It's not that I *must* win. But I want to win. I'm not there to finish second. I'd rather finish tenth than second. I hate the feeling of being so close and not achieving what I set out to do."

Pavin knows the feeling well. In addition to his 15 Tour victories, he's been runner-up 16 times.

To the casual observer, the intensity with which Corey Pavin plays golf suggests he doesn't particularly enjoy himself out on the course. If you get close enough to him as he leaves a green after making bogey, you may hear him muttering to himself like Yosemite Sam, "Stupid, stupid, stupid bogey." You may notice the slight scowl that flashes across his face when the approach shot he planned on sticking within 10 feet of the pin ends up at a thoroughly unacceptable distance. Like 20 feet. You may get the impression that Corey Pavin is frequently angry with himself.

"Actually, I really enjoy myself," Pavin says, smiling. "I thrive on competition and pressure. And my greatest enjoyment comes from seeing how I handle the situation. Can I execute? Can I perform under the circumstances?"

The U.S. Open and Ryder Cup—and the Nissan Open and the Skins Game and the Million Dollar Challenge—provided incontrovertible answers to those questions. Corey

Pavin is one of the rare players whom people say they would want putting (or chipping or whatever the proposition) if their lives depended on it. His name is synonymous with "clutch player."

Winning the Open at Shinnecock Hills, of course, has changed his life forever. Not only have the demands on his time from people like me grown exponentially, not only did he lose the silly moniker "Greatest Player Never to Have Won a Major"—a title, he says, that never bothered him— he's also earned the reputation as being one of the Great Players in golf. These days nobody who follows the game will be surprised if, one day, Corey Pavin is the number-one player in the world. Least of all Corey Pavin.

"I would like nothing more than to win the three other majors," he reveals. "That's one of my goals."

He has built a large and passionate following because the average hacker can identify with him. About someone like Steve Elkington or Ernie Els you might say, "He doesn't even seem to be trying." You would not say that about Corey Pavin. His Chaplinesque jaunty walk; his splayed-knee squat when he lines up a putt, as though he were a frog preparing to spring after a fly; his shouted instructions to the ball as it flies through the air—they all suggest a regular guy very much like you and me grinding out every stroke to keep up with the elegant crowd of Prices and Faldos and Normans.

But more than anything, the reason so many golf fans identify with Corey Pavin is because, next to most of the strapping hunks on Tour, he's small. Not just short, but small, maybe 145 pounds, even with the extra 10 he says he's put on through weight training. (For years his nickname around the practice range was "the jockey.") Corey's stat sheet claims he's 5'9", which may be about as accurate as the one that says Charles Barkley is 6'6". You wouldn't want him on your beach volleyball team. In comparison to the typical touring professional, he is, like his Welsh colleague Ian Woosnam, a wee fellow.

Which makes what he does on a golf course that much more wonderful. I, too, am almost exactly Pavin's height,

117

albeit slightly thicker—and I love the guy. My ex-father-in-law is almost exactly Pavin's height—and he loves the guy. Thousands of other earnest golfers around America stand well on the south side of six feet tall—and they all love the guy, too. This U.S. Open champion is an inspiration to all of us who have at one time or another felt too short to excel at sports, to play with the big boys.

I ask Corey Pavin the elemental woman's magazine question: Does size matter? "Golf is the great equalizer. A six-five guy will usually hit it farther than someone our size. But he'll also usually be more off line. The game isn't a distance contest," Pavin explains. "It's about accuracy, intelligence, course management. It's about handling pressure, about using fine motor skills under pressure. It's about who plays the smartest—which I think is the strength of my game."

Projecting some of my own, well, *short*comings onto him, I ask Pavin if, despite his accuracy and intelligence and all that, he doesn't sometimes feel intimidated by the sheer length of some of the golf courses he faces on a weekly basis.

"Never," he says resolutely. "Oak Hill was supposed to be too long for me. Shinnecock Hills was supposed to be too long for me. I think the results speak for themselves." Pavin says he actually *prefers* difficult golf courses, where any score under par is top-ten material. "You need more patience on hard golf courses, better management of your emotions. When you're constantly facing five- to seven-footers for par, that'll test your nerve and character."

The next day I walk the first round of the tournament with Corey Pavin, studying his attributes, searching, as we all do, for keys to improve my deficient game. Strangely, as if it were a scenario plucked from an episode of *Twilight Zone,* I notice that the gallery following him around the "Blue Monster" course at Doral consists almost exclusively of men more or less my—and Pavin's—size. Purely coincidence, I think, until dropping back a few holes to scout the immense gallery watching the lanky Norman and Davis

Love III: They attract a heterogeneous cross section of the golf-loving public. This is my highly unscientific conclusion: Corey Pavin is a magnet for the under-five-eight crowd.

Watch Corey Pavin's game closely, though, and you realize he's by no means "short" off the tee, just slightly shorter than some of his professional peers. But in the grand scheme of this befuddling game, a few yards here and there do not a champion make. Corey Pavin doesn't overpower a golf course with knockout blows. He sticks and moves. He jabs it into submission.

The man has a beautiful golf game. He's got the consistency of a Tom Kite, the concentration of a Jack Nicklaus, the chipping ability of a Raymond Floyd, and the putting touch of a Ben Crenshaw. But most of all, Corey Pavin has the perfectionist spirit, the competitive fire of a Schwarzkopf or an Eisner or—when the U.S. Open is on the line—a ruthless Shakespearean king.

Of course, you couldn't mistake him for one of that trio. Pavin is the one you'll find on the practice range, searching for an ideal he knows he'll never find: beating balls until he's not quite content.

18

My Pal,
the Touring Pro

In the early 1980s, the best all-around athlete at Nicolet High School in Glendale, Wisconsin, a suburb of Milwaukee, was a small, wiry, red-headed guy named Skip Kendall. We grew up around the corner from each other.

As a youngster, Skip had shown the kind of accelerated physical talents that made people wonder how far he might go in the world of sports. He was fast, the fastest kid at Stormonth Middle School, who blazed past would-be taggers (back when "taggers" played hide-and-seek) with cat-like grace and power. He dominated kickball games and set all kinds of records in Little League baseball (he stole second on me—I was a catcher—virtually every time he reached base), and even won junior bowling and Ping-Pong tournaments. Naturally, inevitably it seemed, when he got older Skip Kendall was the starting point guard on the high-school basketball team, the starting right wing on the soccer team, and could have been the starting center fielder on the baseball team.

Except you never saw Skip on the ballfield during those adolescent summers. While the rest of us were digging out grounders and taking batting practice, Skippy, as he was known, was out at Brown Deer Park, becoming the best golfer ever to grow up in the suburbs of Milwaukee.

Twelve years later I'm carrying Skip Kendall's bag on the PGA Tour.

We're in Moline, Illinois, for the Quad Cities Classic, an event that the Tour's brand-name stars not only seldom attend, but actually tend to belittle in post-match victory interviews: "It's one thing to win some little event like the Quad Cities Classic, but capturing a major—wow, what a thrill!" The truth is, tournaments like the Quad are the heart of the PGA Tour, the weekly grind-out-a-check-and-move-on-to-the-next-stop odyssey that the world's best golfers endure on an almost continuous basis. Almost none of the top 50 players on the money list are in Moline this week. But the next 150 or so are, and most of them are trying to earn enough to stay in the top 125, so they may have the privilege of spending nine weeks straight on the road, moving from motel to motel, competing in slimly publicized tournaments that nobody seems to care about.

Skip Kendall is one of those earnest grinders near the bottom of the list. Until recently, almost nobody knew his name, save for stat-obsessed golf junkies who remembered that he was momentarily atop the leaderboard at the International at Castle Pines a few years ago, before falling to eighth, his best finish in two years on Tour.

Then, a week before Moline, he got hot. At the B.C. Open in Endicott, New York, he led each of the first three days, taking a one-stroke advantage into Sunday's final round, which many meteorologists predicted would be rained out, giving Skip Kendall his first win, $180,000, along with invitations to Augusta and the World Series of Golf and an invigorating respite from athletic anonymity. Alas, the rains didn't come on too strongly, Hal Sutton did (firing a 10-under 61), and Skip settled for seventh. Instead of a Cinderella story, it was back to the office.

When I meet him at the Oakwood Country Club, site of the Q.C.C. and minutes from the Mississippi River, he looks as he did when we were teenagers: slim, wiry, unprepossessing. It's hard to imagine him driving a golf ball 270 yards or more, which he does with surprising regularity. It's hard

122

to imagine that in any given week he's capable of shooting the same scores as Faldo and Funk, Lehman and Lowery. Or anyone else out there.

For the first few months that Skip Kendall was on the PGA Tour, I spent many anxious Friday and Saturday mornings tracking his results in the sports-page box scores. How odd it was to see Kendall ... 35-34—69 right next to Couples ... 33-36—69, or to Love or a dozen other golfing luminaries. I still can't quite fathom that a guy from down the street is one of the best 100 or so players in the world. Another boyhood teammate, Lance Painter, pitches for the Colorado Rockies. I was his first catcher in Little League. And now he's throwing curve balls to Mike Piazza and Barry Bonds. It all seems so unreal.

The ethereal wonder of it all vanishes the moment I sling Skip's bag over my shoulder. The thing must weigh close to a hundred pounds with all his clubs and balls and rain gear in it, and no matter how cool it feels to be inside the ropes, chatting on the range with the golf gods we see on television each weekend, proximity to the game's most accomplished players does not make the load any lighter.

"Let's go, looper," Skip says to me, ambling toward the practice green. "We've got work to do."

For the typical professional caddie, "work" means carrying the pro's bag; keeping the clubheads, grips, and balls clean; reporting accurate yardage; knowing everything about the course that can possibly be known (hidden hazards to avoid, the peculiar slope of each green); and generally attending to the pro's idiosyncrasies from the moment the boss arrives at the course until he departs.

For a touring professional, "work" means hitting hundreds of practice balls a day, stroking dozens of putts, and conditioning his muscles and mind to perform under pressure. Even when you play golf better than almost everyone on the planet, you still tweak, you still refine. You try to get better.

Skip Kendall is intimately acquainted with this process. "I've always been the kind of person that started sort of slowly and gradually improved," he says, draining three 12-footers in a row. "I don't usually have instant success. But I keep trying to progress to the next level."

In high school, Skip never managed to win Wisconsin's statewide tournament; he finished second, twice. In college, on scholarship at UNLV, he had what he describes as "a mediocre career," failing to win even a conference tournament. (On summers home from school, he successfully trounced the local competition, winning most everything in the micro-universe that is Milwaukee golf.) He knew 100 guys who were better than him. And yet, after graduating with a degree in business education, for some ineluctable reason, Kendall thought he might have a shot at being a professional golfer. "It's a dream, a dream that everyone says can't be done," he says, lining up a practice putt while I crouch behind the hole, imitating the other caddies. "I wanted to try."

From 1987 through 1991, Skip Kendall attended the Tour's dreaded Q-School. He failed to qualify every year.

In 1988, after sampling a few mini-tour events in Arizona, where a top-five finish might get your entry fee back, Skip moved to Orlando with the intention of playing on one of the plentiful mini-tours there. Barely able to afford entry fees, let alone live on the meager prizes he hoped to win, Kendall worked as a waiter, two shifts a day. Between the lunch and dinner hours, still clad in white shirt and bow-tie ("They took too long to take on and off"), he would retire to a nearby field with his shag bag, beating balls until it was time to go back to folding napkins. Though there's something seductively romantic about this scenario—like the farm boy who teaches himself to become an NFL quarterback by throwing ears of corn during the harvest—Skip says his practice routine was simply a matter of logistics. "I didn't have the time, and I definitely didn't have the money, to play the resort courses. It wasn't fun being out there in a field, but I hoped someday it would pay off."

It did. He won the fourth mini-tour event he entered.

By 1989 he started making big enough checks to quit the restaurant job. By 1990 he was competing in nearly 100 mini-tourneys a year. And by 1991 he was earning around $60,000 from playing golf.

Then something wonderful happened to his career: He earned a spot in the Macon, Georgia, Hogan (now Buy.com) Tour event through a Monday qualifier, in which 200 hungry pros battled for 14 spots in the big show. He placed third in the main event and went on to win enough prize money to earn a conditional Hogan Tour card. "When they sent me the money clip [the Tour's identifying badge], it was a pretty emotional moment," he recalls.

Skip finished 23rd on the money list, guaranteeing himself a spot on the 1993 Nike Tour. Instead, he went back to the PGA Tour Q-School, where, disastrously, he shot an opening-round 79. "I had a hole in one of my shoes," he remembers. "I asked a certain major shoe company for a replacement pair. They wouldn't have anything to do with me." Five rounds later, after a sterling final-round 67, Skip Kendall was the Q-School co-medalist. And a member of the PGA Tour.

Now companies like Titleist and Orlimar pay him to use their products. And boyhood teammates want to schlep his bag.

Jack Nicklaus has said, "I never thought a caddie helps very much. He can hurt you, though."

When Skip plays his first practice round at Oakwood on a drizzly Tuesday morning, I am by his side, with Jack's words of discouragement ringing in my mind, trying mightily not to embarrass myself or my pro. The other caddies, a swarthy bunch who don't welcome outsiders warmly, eye me warily, as though I'm a scab opportunist crossing their unspoken picket line. Though most Tour caddies earn as little as $400 a week plus bonuses (five percent of earnings, seven percent for a top 10, 10 percent for a win), out of which they must pay their own travel and meal expenses, they covet their jobs ferociously and do not suffer dilettantes kindly.

Arriving at Skip's ball after his first teeshot, the other

caddies eavesdrop as Kendall asks for his yardage to the front of the green. "All right, looper. Whaddya got?" I thumb through "the book," a meticulously mapped schematic of each hole, find the appropriate landmark, and count off the steps. It's only a practice round, and Skip and the other pros—Mike Brisky, Willie Wood, and Barry Cheesman—aren't even playing their customary skins game, but I'm as nervous as a Tour rookie standing over a four-foot par putt to force a playoff. "Buck thirty-two," I say with something less than certainty.

"Dave, is that what you've got?" Skip asks another caddie.

"Yeah. More or less."

My par putt has dropped. After a few holes, I'm initiated into the caddie fraternity when, mortifyingly, I "lose" one of my pro's head covers, only to find that one of my bag-toting colleagues has stuffed it in his pocket. (Three holes later, I return the favor and officially become one of the guys.) The caddies teach me the finer points of the job, such as don't let the bag drop while somebody's swinging and always stand outside your pro's peripheral vision, and the Cardinal Rule of Caddying: When your pro eagles from a greenside bunker, it's "we" who did it; when he snap-hooks a drive into the rough, it's "he."

Several times I taste the panic of confusion (*where's the small bush that's supposed to be 168 yards from the green?*) and the joy of inclusion, as when my pro—not my boyhood neighbor, my *pro*—asks my opinion on the break of a putt or which club seems best given the sloppy conditions. For a few moments during Skip's rainy practice round, I feel like I'm actually part of something, that I'm his teammate again after 15 years, working with him toward another victory.

And though he shoots 70-74 and misses the cut by one at Moline, does likewise the next week at the Buick Challenge, and finishes his year far down on the money list, I'm still proud of him. Even though he has to return to Q-School and toil another year in virtual anonymity, Skip Kendall is still the kid around the block who made the big time. Even though he fails to win PGA Tour events no matter what kind of lead he takes into Sunday, Skip Kendall is still in the big show, where millions of other dreamers wish they could be.

He's still my hero.

19

THE VINNY

If you need incontrovertible evidence that life is not fair, look no further than Vince Gill.

He's sold about a jillion albums, won nearly as many major recording-industry awards (okay, only 68, including 11 Grammys and 17 Country Music Association honors, more than any artist in history), and regularly inspires in his listeners the kind of unabashed joy usually reserved for puppies and newborn children.

And he carries a 1-handicap on the golf course.

That's not fair.

It's not fair to sing as beautifully as he does *and* play the impossible game of golf so effortlessly. As they say in the land of steel guitars and warbling fiddles, it just ain't *right*. When did he make his deal with the devil? Where's the trade-off that normally accompanies the inheritance of one-in-a-million talents? Look around. To be blessed with a divine voice often means accepting excess baggage (hello, Luciano!), the absence of sight (think Stevie Wonder), or a predilection for bouts of frightening nastiness (Frank Sinatra and Kathleen Battle, to name but two). Vince Gill is *nice*. Vince Gill is nice and sings angelically *and* plays golf about as well as any amateur worthy of his oversized titanium driver.

Most folks would settle for just one piece of the pie. The average guitar picker knocking around Nashville? He wouldn't mind shooting a hundred for nine holes so long as you promised him that grown men would weep at the sound of his sweet tenor. The average hacker? He wouldn't mind if he had to carry a tune in a bucket so long as you promised him Elkington's swing and Crenshaw's putting stroke.

Vince Gill doesn't have to settle. Which is not only not fair, but also slightly confusing. Here's a fellow for whom smugness should come about as easily as a wicked slice does for the rest of us. Here's a fellow who, by all rights, should inspire envy, jealousy, and incessant back-stabbing.

But let's be clear: When it comes to Nashville, Vince Gill is revered. He's a good guy, as opposed to a bad boy, which, as some other country music stars will attest, is one way of marketing yourself. Vince Gill's musical persona is good boy. So is his civic persona. He sings like an angel, and, according to everyone who knows him, especially anyone who has anything to do with golf, he conducts himself like one, too.

When it comes to golf, particularly junior golf, Vince Gill is *the man*. This is manifested most prominently in an annual Pro-Celebrity Invitational golf tournament Vince hosts each summer in Nashville. It's called the "Vinny," and most folks in the South affectionately call it the first "country major." For two days, Vince and his friends play golf and sign autographs and pose for snapshots in front of tens of thousands of bedazzled fans. PGA Tour players like John Daly, Fuzzy Zoeller, and Payne Stewart often show up, as do other luminaries from the world of sports, like Super Bowl-winning quarterbacks Jim McMahon and Brett Favre, the latter a long-hittin' Southern boy. So do many superstars of country music, including singers who need only one name (Garth, Reba) to be recognized by anyone who drives a pickup truck and wears cowboy boots. This kind of drawing power translates into a stellar bottom line: In eight years Vince and his pals have raised more than

$2 million for Tennessee junior golf. Yeah, Bubba, they tend to like Vince Gill 'round these parts.

The bulk of the Vinny's largesse has gone toward the Little Course, a wee nine-hole facility with country club-quality tees, fairways, and greens, located on the grounds of Golf House, the home of the Tennessee Golf Association. It's a perfect track for budding golfers to learn the game, and on the Little Course you see many families out for a stroll. Fathers pass down hard-earned wisdom to their sons and daughters, embodying "golf values" that these days are more often talked about than honored. Children here discover a game they will either despise or play for a lifetime, and it's mostly thanks to a country-music singer named Vince.

The practice putting green at Golf House is already named for Vince Gill, but those who administer junior golf in this state are still looking for ways to adequately express their appreciation for all he's done. On the eve of the 1998 Vinny, Golf House dedicated a bronze statue to Vince's dad, Judge J. Stan Gill, who died in 1997. The sculpture, which stands outside the front entrance, depicts a father with a guiding hand on his boy's shoulder—a boy, it turns out, modeled after Vincent Gill at eight years old.

As his soon-to-be new wife, the singer Amy Grant, reads a devotional passage about remembrance, Vince Gill, now in his 40s, sits beside his own teen-age daughter and wipes away the tears. This statue dedication is a resolutely *country* affair, with plenty of down-home speech-making, live guitar performances, and the title song from Vince's CD, "The Key of Life" (also dedicated to Stan Gill), playing on the public-address system. Choking back sobs, Vince tells the assembly that his favorite part of the day was driving up to Golf House and seeing a skinny boy on the Little Course, slapping around a golf ball. "The kid offered me two shots per nine. Said, 'We'll play for your car.'"

It's no accident that Vince Gill is enormously charming, modest, self-effacing, and grateful for everything he has accomplished. "My daddy told me," Vince explained to the crowd, "that none of your fame or money means anything if you don't stay the same."

He's done well staying the same. And people adore him for that. When he gives a free concert at the Grand Ole Opry after the first round of the Vinny, the night is an uninterrupted lovefest, with the mayor of Nashville announcing he will recommend that the parks council rename a municipal course the Vinny Links and former First Hacker President Bush expressing his adulation via videotape.

This barrage of affection carries over to the golf course, where the celebrity singer transforms himself into a celebrity athlete. He hits the ball about as far as anyone who doesn't make his living playing golf. He's got every shot in the bag. And he can putt some, too. The guy's a player.

I know this because I was paired with Vince Gill in the 1998 edition of the Vinny. Nothing in the realm of my golf experience was quite so intimidating—not putting with Lee Janzen, not hitting chip shots with Raymond Floyd, not standing on the first tee with Laura Davies. Not even attempting to make my opening drive at the Old Course, with dozens of grizzled locals watching through unblinking eyes. Nothing in golf has been quite as daunting as playing golf with Vince Gill, the Saint of Nashville, in front of 10,000 of his faithful flock.

When we met at the Golf Club of Tennessee, a gorgeous Tom Fazio layout and home to the Vinny, Vince was already doing his best to balance his golf game (which he takes very seriously) with his celebrity status (which he takes less seriously), alternately beating practice balls on the range and signing hundreds—thousands?—of autographs. Riding with him in an electric buggy to our first hole was slightly scary, a halting crawl through a pen-wielding telephoto-lens-prodding human gauntlet of fans, all eager to get a piece of him, a tangible bit of proof that they had some sort of contact, no matter how fleeting, with quadruple-platinum Vince.

I asked him what's harder, singing in a stadium or teeing it up at the Vinny. "It's no contest," Gill says, shaking his head in disbelief. "As I've done better as a performer, I've had a harder time playing good golf. It scares me to death. Tell you the truth, I hate it."

So why put himself through the torture?

"I guess I'm not afraid to look like an idiot in front of thousands of people," Gill says, laughing. "At this tournament, I just let go of any expectations I have of playing well. I sign autographs and mingle and have a good time."

Thanks to this generous attitude, each walk from tee to fairway took forever. Each walk from fairway to green took forever. And each walk from green to the next tee took forever and then some. But if it hadn't, the members of our sevensome (since it's Vince's tournament, he can bend the rules when he wants a couple of his buddies from the world of country music to join him on the links) wouldn't have had the opportunity to witness the kind of libidinal frenzy that you might have thought went out with bobby sox and the Beatles.

On the first tee, a security guard murmured to Vince that a woman had been standing against the gallery ropes for about three hours, begging for a chance to take a picture with Mr. Vinny. Apparently, she was a big fan—a *big* fan. Seems her baby is named after Vince.

When Vince invited the lady (and her baby) onto the tee for a quick snapshot, she came close to fainting on the spot. Luckily, the sobs of joy that wracked her body kept her sentient, and she was able to proffer her infant to Vince, so that he might sign the lad. "Sign the *baby?*" Vince asked.

"Well, his shirt, then," the lady replied.

Safely down the fairway, Vince told us, his playing partners, that when he dies, if anyone puts a Sharpie pen in his coffin, he'll surely come back from the grave and use it to slash the guy's throat.

Even with the constant distractions, Vince has got a ton of game. But if you believe that someone's golf swing mirrors his personality, then it's not the game you might expect. Listen to his records, smooth and soothing as warm honey dribbling down a slice of freshly baked cornbread.

133

Then watch him swing. You're thinking Ernie Els, but you're seeing Nick Price.

"Tempo has always escaped me," Vince Gill, master of rhythm, admits. "I'm a thrasher, a real handsy player—I guess that carries over from music, from pickin' the guitar. I just like to hit the golf ball real quick."

And long. The only member of our team who drove it anywhere near Vince was Anthony Rodriguez, and he plays on the Nike Tour.

❖ ❖ ❖

Vince Gill started playing golf when he was six, back in Oklahoma. He discovered a talent for the game at just about the same time he discovered a talent for music, and for many of his childhood years he thought he might want to be a professional golfer. That didn't work out, so he settled for being a music superstar instead. "I don't think most people realize how good these pros are," Gill says, referring to the dozens of highly sponsored athletes who visit the Vinny each year. "If I applied myself to golf like I did to music, could I have been a pro? I doubt it. I've had a scratch handicap. But is 'zero' as good as it gets? Handicaps for most of these guys would be like plus five. So there's a world of difference between someone like me and them."

Still, he plays golf every day when he's on the road, swapping concert tickets for greens fees. Vince Gill tells me that he's shot three 66s in his life. "But I've also shot up to eighty-five and every number in between," he jokes.

I've never shot a 66. (I almost never shoot 76.) But on the 15th hole, when I stick a 7-iron within four feet of the pin and receive an enthusiastic high-five and a "I-guess-the-press-ain't-all-bad" comment from the tournament host, I know why I love this game. But what about Vince Gill? Why does he so love golf?

"I wish I knew why I love the game," Vince says to me, thinking hard.

"It's like your mama," he says. "You just *do*."

HAVE CLUBS
WILL TRAVEL

20

Barging Through Scotland

Were there no such animal as Canadians, the Scots might easily wear the crown of the friendliest people on Earth. They're quick with a smile, quick with a wry remark, and even quicker to join you for a dose of liquid refreshment. Everyone has theories why this should be. The complicated ones involve Scotland's notoriously fickle weather, which, the reasoning goes, forces its residents to be eternal optimists. The simple explanation, according to my expatriate Scottish neighbor in Los Angeles, is, "We Scots are a nation of happy drunks."

Call me biased, but I suspect Scottish congeniality can somehow be traced to golf. A nation that can invent any activity as preposterously wonderful as our beloved sport—not to mention curling and that game where they toss tree trunks end-over-end—has got to have a finely developed sense of humor.

Case in point: I'm in the Highlands, preparing to embark on a week-long cruise through duffer's elysium, stopping each day to play the esteemed and sacred courses upon which the game was invented. At the local course in Inverness, a mere 5,800 yards from the men's tees—nearly 1,000 yards shorter than my home course in Hollywood—the starter asks me if I have a handicap. I tell him yes. He says, "Okay." I ask him if he wants to know what it is? He shrugs. "Nay." As I head for the first hole, he advises me to play from the yellow markers, reducing this already short layout by another couple hundred yards. Has he judged me a hopeless hacker already? I look at the scorecard: The first, a par-4, is only 301 yards. Sensing my dismay, he says, "Ye dinna wan' ah play from the whites t'day. Ye'll be havin' all the golf ye need."

Standing on the tee, I understand. The wind is approximately 35 mph and it's directly in my face. I tee up my ball and laugh.

Everyone always talks about how golf is a different game over in Scotland, how Americans are usually unprepared for the dramatic changes in topography and meteorology once they leave their sedate, exquisitely manicured, emerald carpets back home. But this is ridiculous. I have to lean forward merely to stand up straight. If this wind were circulating off the Florida coast, they'd be giving a name to it.

Frightened to hit a driver—the ball may fly too high and end up behind me, crashing into the pro shop—I take a 2-iron and blast a low screamer into the gale. It goes about 130 yards, mostly on the roll. Which, here in the land of bump-and-run, qualifies as a magnificent shot. I wipe the tears from my eyes and embark on my inaugural round of Scottish golf.

The first four holes are magic: a 2-iron stiff to the pin on a 128-yard par-3; chip shots that run for miles; lofty pitches that begin out of bounds and ride the wind back to the green. It's hard not to read too much *Golf in the Kingdom* mysticism into the rightness of every stroke, as though I'm a pilgrim who has finally found his sanctuary. But playing alone, toting my bag on my shoulder, gauging distances without benefit of yardage markers or sprinkler heads or pin-placement sheets, I feel as though I'm experiencing the game in a vaguely primal state, in a way that turns even the most sensible cynic into a blubbering spiritual mess. Par, birdie, par, par. All is right with the world.

Nothing is as it should be, but somehow (recovered memory? past lives?) it all makes sense. Putts must be read not so much by the break of the green as by the direction of the wind. Approach irons you would normally fire at the flag in America must be landed at least 20 yards short of the green, onto solid brown fairways that bounce the ball like wooden springboards. Nearly all manner of golf shots must be kept low.

On the 18th, a downwind 461-yard par-4, I reach the green with driver, 9-iron.

Playing golf in Scotland teaches you not to get greedy, to dance with the course, not attack it. Zen, and all that. You must resign yourself to 5s on some par-4s. You must prepare for the weather and land to punish imperfect strokes. But on the other hand, you get to rejoice when seemingly bad shots become good ones, and good ones are lovelier than you thought possible.

After one round of Scottish golf, I feel as though I could return home and write a fantastical treatise about the life lessons taught by an inscrutable golfer-philosopher who makes holes-in-one in the middle of the night, using a varnished tree branch.

❖ ❖ ❖

In its former life as a Dutch trading vessel on the Danube and Rhine, the 36-meter M.V. *Vertrouwen* ("Faithful One"), christened in 1931, probably carried stuff like sacks of grain and used tires. Today, the barge is a luxury hotel ship, ferrying up to eight extraordinarily pampered passengers and five meticulous crew members through some of the most exquisite countryside ever put on a postcard. From April through October, the *Vertrouwen* cruises Scotland's Caledonian Canal, between Inverness and Fort William, traversing Loch Ness on the way. Several of these cruises each year are designated "Golf Cruises," which, in the grand scheme of life, may be the noblest purpose the fair boat has ever served.

139

At the first-day's reception, passengers are drowned in champagne and single-malt whisky, setting an appropriately intoxicated tone for the week's festivities. (In the best Scottish tradition, the barge's self-serve bar is always open.) Captain Trevor Jones and his mate, Rita, tell us that the ship should feel like a water-borne country home, where the food, service, and comfort are first-class but the mood is informal. Admittedly, drinking good French wines and Portuguese port and more single-malt nectar than a normally abstemious American ought to has a way of smoothing out rough edges. But I believe I am sober enough to report that the Joneses and their crew have mastered the difficult task of anticipating their guests' every need in advance, of being solicitous without stooping to obsequiousness, of hosting superbly. Their proper English accents also have a way of tricking you into thinking you're in a Merchant-Ivory production.

Knowing in the morning that we will be visiting Royal Dornoch, considered one of the greatest links on Earth, I spend the night looking out my cabin window, hoping the sun has risen. Since we are merely four degrees latitude south of Juneau, Alaska, the sun barely even sets.

Dornoch is a classical, completely natural course whose character changes with the wind and, like the Old Course at St. Andrews, the placement of the flags on the vast greens. Set on the edge of Embo Bay, on public land, the course is a municipal meeting place, where golfers mingle with residents walking their dogs and children riding bikes through the fairways. When we arrive, after a brief van ride through countryside inhabited, it seems, solely by livestock, the day is unusually sunny, with only a gentle puff of wind to cool the air. This isn't right, I think, fondling my freshly purchased rain pants, rain shirt, and rain shell. Golf in Scotland is supposed to be played in gales, with various forms of precipitation pelting your face. Retelling your round here is supposed to resemble a war story. The day is too perfect. The locals, squinting at the sun, seem to be in a mild state of shock.

Though the dreaded gorse gobbles up a couple of way-ward balls and a hidden fairway bunker or two produce a number of bogeys, Royal Dornoch provides me with per-haps the most charming round of golf I've ever enjoyed. Utterly natural, undisturbed by the hand of man, its im-mense mounds, dramatic drop-offs, waist-high "whin" (gorse without prickers), and sloping fairways harder than most American greens make Royal Dornoch a singular ex-perience. As all the golf guides suggest, you must bounce your approach shot well in front of the green and you must know how to chip. Accuracy off the tee is richly rewarded; wildness is punished. Simple.

After a string of pars, I remark to my caddie that Royal Dornoch strikes me as a unique, memorable golf course, but not a particularly hard one.

He smiles and points to the sea, which is visible from most of the holes. "Ye come on the one day a' the yer wi' nay wind." If I had played the course two days earlier, he promises, I would have thought Dornoch the hardest course in the world.

My 83 suddenly seems like a welcome gift from the lairds of Scottish golf. As I walk off the 18th wishing the day would never end, I realize no matter what score you shoot here, it really doesn't matter much. Imperfect play cannot blemish a perfect golf course. Golf in the kingdom, indeed.

❖ ❖ ❖

This is one of the advantages of floating through Scot-land on a luxury barge: Instead of heading to the 19th hole for a warm pitcher of beer and a game of gin rummy, we return to a floating hotel, where poached salmon, lemon soufflé, and more than a few wee drams of the local bev-erage await us. Then off to our cozy berths for golfy dreams.

❖ ❖ ❖

Set on the Moray firth, the Nairn Golf Club boasts some of the finest putting surfaces in Scotland. The fairways are said to be slightly softer than most seaside courses, though I would hardly know, missing all but two of them. The rough at Nairn is what I'm familiar with. On my horticultural tour of the grasses of the Scottish Highlands, I encounter spiny gorse, wiry heather, and wispy "couch" grass, all of which I manage to visit with alarming frequency, despite a remarkable dearth of wind. With the breeze down, Nairn, like many links, is largely defenseless. Hit it crooked, though, and triple digits becomes a distinct possibility.

My sweet caddie, David, 67, whose encouraging words sound like music, like extemporaneous poetry, says, "The heather is quite bonny win sum'un hands ye a boonch, but ye dinna wanna hit fra' it." Instead, he counsels, "Ye wanna hit smack on, wi' bags o' power." Avoid Nairn's fairway bunkers, he warns, "less we be spendin' all day in't." Of missed putts and pushed drives, he says, "'Twas bad luck then." When I take three to get out of a dry ditch running through the second fairway, David has no comment, only a resigned shrug. We both laugh.

On a sublime summer day, highlighted by an unexpected exhibition by the Red Arrows flying team, I shoot a miserable never-made-a-putt-over-10-feet 94—and love every inept minute of it.

After golf, the barge cruises 13 miles down the Caledonian Canal, from Inverness to Foyers, passing verdant countryside brimming with plants, animals, life. The livestock—cattle, sheep, goats—all graze together. Only the pigs have their own ghetto. Every acre we float by teems with furry creatures that you either want to hug or make into a sweater.

Scotland is a terrifically green country. You can almost smell the chlorophyll in the air. The entire Highlands region looks like a golf course, and the golf courses look like somebody's farm with 18 flags in it. Which makes you think: Isn't there something perverse about finding golf courses in Palm Springs, Las Vegas, Arizona? In the desert? What do the Scots make of all this irrigation and recycled water business? Their courses are the product of a temperate climate, plenty of rain, and, in the early days, industrious sheep looking for a place to hide from storms. They don't even water their fairways; if the ground turns brown and hard and unseemly, you don't worry about the aesthetic shortcomings. You play a useful bump-and-run and get on with it, laddie.

I ask my caddie one day what kind of grass is used on the greens. Certainly not Bermuda. Bent, maybe? He tells me the greens are simply "meadow grass," the same plant that grows to waist level along the fairways. "Regular grass," he says. "We just cut it shorter on the greens."

❖ ❖ ❖

Cruising through Scotland's splendid desolation, we spy a nest of osprey tucked into the pines on the towering hillsides. There are more birds here than people. Only as the *Vertrouwen* passes through little locks do we see any townsfolk, who come out to say hello and watch our vessel get raised or lowered a few feet. On deck, with binoculars in one hand and a wee dram in the other, I study my scorecards from Inverness, Dornoch, and Nairn, trying to decide which of the hole titles I like best. The Old Course, I discover, is not the only links to have a "Road" hole, nor is calling the 18th "Home" an American innovation. Stateside, however, you'll not find holes called "Gizzen Briggs" and "Tarbat Ness" and "Ben Wyvis." And where else but Scotland can you play holes like the unpronounceable "Achareidh" or the eloquently descriptive "Long"?

❖ ❖ ❖

We reach the storied Loch Ness in the morning. On its verdant banks we see soaring buzzards and herds of stags, which sit in great groups of 100 or more, chewing their cuds like cattle, staring incredulously. (In what some passengers

143

perceive as unfortunate timing and others as a clever culinary joke, Sally, the *Vertrouwen*'s superb chef, prepares venison that evening.) You half expect a cast of spear-waving thousands to come charging over the hills. The scene is almost too storybook to be true.

Driving in the ship's van through tiny towns that make you wonder what you're doing living in a city of nine million people, we arrive at the 100-year-old Boat of Garten golf club, a scenic inland layout that compensates for a lack of sea wind with narrow tilting fairways, blind approach shots, and more hills than Castle Pines. It's a short course— less than 5,800 yards—that makes you question why you're not consistently shooting par. The 15th at Boat of Garten is probably the most peculiar hole you'll ever play. You either attempt to drive the green, surrounded by "broom" on either side, or lay-up in front of a cavernous gully. It's the first time I ever play a par-4 with a wedge off the tee followed by a 7-iron to the green (and almost certainly the last).

I make several birdies, a bunch of pars, and a few complete disasters. Nicklaus-in-hell-like, it takes me four to extricate myself from one particularly nasty bunker, and three more to emerge from a gnarly tract of forest. My 70-something turns into a 91. Inexplicably, I am not the least bit unhappy.

Afterward, I share a lager shandy—one part beer, one part lemonade—with my caddie. Meanwhile, Captain Jones, a stout-hearted fellow who likes his ale warm, neat, and very tall, seems genuinely dismayed that one of the passengers should quench his thirst with such a diluted spirit. "All that water can't be good for you," he chides. "Please, let me get you a whisky."

Returning to the barge, we traverse rolling meadows and sheltered valleys that look like sets from *Braveheart*. Alistair, our historical guide and *Vertrouwen* crew member, who is a dead ringer for Janitor Willie from "The Simpsons," says that, in fact, both the Mel Gibson vehicle and *Rob Roy* were filmed simultaneously in the Glen Nevis area, farther south. For weeks at a time, Alistair says, he encountered traffic delays and radio-toting twits. "And not once did I see so much as a starlet's ankle!" he adds.

Floating the entire length of Loch Ness, not once do I see so much as a dorsal fin—or anything else that might suggest a prehistoric creature lurking in the depths. But I do notice several dozen baronial estates on the distant banks that will make splendid country homes when I manage to sock away a spare million or three.

Loch Ness terminates beneath a Benedictine abbey at a little one-pub, five-lock, 500-person town called Fort Augustus. After hitting a ceremonial drive into Loch Ness for the sake of metaphysical symbolism—or, more likely, because I am slightly stewed—I ride one of the barge's old bicycles to the diminutive Fort Augustus municipal golf course. In addition to typical hazards like bunkers and marshlands, the course offers the moving obstacle of grazing sheep, most of which favor the sweet grass around the greens. There's also a peculiar but necessary Local Rule: "A ball lying on sheep's wool, or on or made dirty by sheep droppings, may be lifted and cleaned without penalty."

Similarly, at Newtonmore, an inland park-style course I play the next day, cattle and sheep go about their business behind several of the tees. As I prepare to hit a drive on the inward nine, my backswing is interrupted by a prodigious belch, offered up by an oblivious Angus. Ah, golf in its natural state!

Since my caddie at Newtonmore is an earnest 11-year-old who can only guess at yardage—like every other course in Scotland, Newtonmore is bereft of precisely measured sprinkler heads or 150-yard bushes—I play by eye alone. Occasionally I'm within 20 yards of being correct. Ah, primal golf!

My playing partner, Tony, a *Vertrouwen* crew member and the cruise golf manager, manages to find some of Newtonmore's highest grass on one unfortunate hole, subsequently teaching me the peculiarly British oath, "Oh, come now, you silly sausage!" Later, when my ball finds the currents of the mighty River Spey, I picture myself as a giggling knackwurst, and I don't feel so bad.

Our last leg of barging takes us from Laggan to Banavie, through Loch Lochy, the "Dark Goddess." As the boat approaches Ben Nevis, the tallest peak in the U.K., songs from *Brigadoon* spin through my head. Back when my high-school drama department performed the musical, lyrics like "The mist of May is in the *gloamin'* / There's lazy music in the rill / So take my hand and let's go roamin' / Through the heather on the hill" meant nothing to me. Today, I'm still not exactly sure what the *gloamin'* is, but looking at the fog-shrouded mountains, hearing a lonely sheep bleating in the mist, somehow I know what the song is trying to say.

Our trip through Scotland concludes at the Gleneagles Hotel, one of the finest—and most expensive—resorts in the world. For those who have yet to discover the joys of the Great Game or need some time to figure out their nagging slice, Gleneagles offers an eclectic array of diversions. Guests may enjoy all manner of racquet sports, croquet, fly fishing, horseback riding, four-wheel driving, clay target shooting (at the Jackie Stewart Shooting School), and, remarkably, the medieval sport of falconry, in which majestic birds of prey perch on your gloved hand, ready to light off in search of hares. If my professional duties did not require otherwise, I might easily spend an entire stay at Gleneagles flitting from falconry school to shamelessly rich meals to a grand hotel room back to my pals, the eagles and the hawks—and never pine for a single sand trap.

Alas, Gleneagles is home to 63 holes of the best golf Europe; to miss any of them would be akin to visiting Paris and dining exclusively at Pizza Hut.

There's the Wee course, nine par-3s that require nearly every club in your bag. (The adjacent Golf Academy, probably the most advanced learning facility in Scotland, teaches you how to swing them.) There's the Monarch's course, a Jack Nicklaus design that reeks of American characteristics like five tee boxes and paved cart paths. (The Scots, I'm told, are crazy about the carts; it's Calvinist Americans like me who frown upon this concession to modernity.) And there are the originals.

Set amid the kind of undulating Perthshire countryside that no amount of bulldozers and cranes could ever re-create, the oldest courses at Gleneagles, the Queen's and the King's, built by the prolific James Braid in the 1920s, are everything a golf course should be: beautiful, challenging, provocative, amusing, and peaceful. Actually, I can only assume the front nine of the Queen's are all those things, since the beginning of my round is played in a soupy fog that reduces visibility to 30 yards or so. (In Scotland, only lightning interrupts a round. Otherwise, "Play on!") Never have I appreciated an expert companion so much as during my Queen's round, teeing off into oblivion. My caddie, Richard, 30, a somber, thoroughly professional veteran of 14 years, watches my ball disappear in the mist, makes a calculation or two, and marches off directly to where the elusive orb has come to rest. His skill is nearly as impressive as the endless vistas to which I'm treated once the clouds roll off.

No matter how lovely or exotic the locale, eventually you get pangs for home. Eventually you say, "Thailand's been great, but I've had enough curry already—let's get out of here." Few places make you wish never to leave. Scotland is one of those places. During my last round at Gleneagles—my last round in Scotland—I feel the same bittersweet remorse Arnold Palmer must have felt walking up the 18th at Oakmont: it's hard to say goodbye to a place and a game and a feeling you so love.

My playing partner that final day is a local fellow, Hugh, who has just returned from a week-long golf vacation in Myrtle Beach. I tell him how much I've enjoyed barging through Scotland. He tells me how much he enjoyed visiting America. I tell him how I've enjoyed meeting so many nice Scotsmen. He says the same about his new American friends. I tell him how blissful the golf has been here on the ancient turf.

147

He does not even try to return the compliment. He merely nods and smiles. "Aye, lad," he says, surveying the land around us. "Thar's noothin' like it in the warld."

21

THE LAND
OF CAMELOT

Americans, especially golfing Americans, tend to favor tourist destinations that don't seem like tourist destinations because, we convince ourselves, they seem not to have too many tourists in them. We like to trailblaze, to discover what the travel magazines claim are "undiscovered" places. "Unspoiled" is a big deal to us. When we journey abroad with our golf clubs, we want to see another world, another land, not thousands of people who look like our next-door neighbors, sound like our office-mate, and behave like our children.

So I should tell you right off that Cornwall, in the southwest of England, is swarming with tourists.

Funny thing is, though, they're nothing like your friends back home. No, the tourists in Cornwall have accents worthy of the Royal Shakespeare Company, enjoy afternoon tea, and use the phrase "He's a fine old chap, Simon is" without any intended irony.

That is to say, the tourists in Cornwall are mostly British. The locals call them "holiday makers," a term that connotes men and women of action, vacationers not content to stand idly by while their leisure time expires. In the pursuit of making holidays, *good* holidays, these vacationing Brits—from London, Manchester, wherever—descend upon

Cornwall in coaches (buses), caravans (mobile homes), and occasionally their weekends-only Ferraris (very fast cars), searching dutifully for the quaint stopped-in-time England that would seem to exist only in the imagination.

Based on some painstaking research I too conducted not long ago, making a successful Cornish holiday primarily involves quaffing prodigious amounts of English ale and chasing a little white ball around ancient sand dunes, while a 40-mph wind threatens to blow everything not nailed down into Wales.

Yes, Cornwall is where many vacationing Brits come to play golf.

And why not? Cornwall is so pungently green you can almost taste the sweet Vitamin B in the air. Where sheep and cattle aren't roaming the hilly countryside, there are stone farmhouses and impossibly cute cottages, dating from medieval times. Indeed, this part of Britain, the residents say, is the Land of King Arthur. Now, some other, less beautiful, more tourist-hungry counties say *they* were the real home of the Round Table. But Cornwall, according to my sources—slightly inebriated local farmers and craftsmen enjoying their fourth pint of the evening—is the real deal. I'll say this: Were it not for the presence of diesel-powered tractors and the occasional coach filled with English tourists—I mean, *holiday makers*—you could easily imagine scads of gallant knights galloping across the verdant moors in defense of God, country, and flaxen-haired damsels.

This is all to say that Cornwall is one of the most achingly beautiful places on Earth. And, thus, a particularly wonderful locale to play golf.

You can fly to London, transfer to Plymouth or Newquay, and follow the lead of the holiday makers. Or you can do what I did, which is book a week-long golf package with an outfit called Halcyon Days Vacations—"A Time of Peace and Happiness," the brochure says—a company owned and operated by residents of Cornwall who are most eager to show off their beloved homeland to visiting Americans. (And everyone else, too.) Your week in Cornwall includes five rounds of golf, all meals and adult beverages, the services of an expert guide-driver-raconteur-drinking mate, and accommodations at the London Inn, a 17th-century post house with three charming *en suite* rooms on the second floor and the center of the universe on the first floor.

The local pub, I mean. The London Inn sits stolidly where it has sat for hundreds of years, in the middle of a little Cornish village called St. Neot (pronounced *suh-nit* after you've had a few), home to perhaps 800 surpassingly friendly residents. Many of them live down remote lanes far from the manic bustle of the town center, where you'll find a church and three businesses—a grocery-post office, a petrol station, and the London Inn. When the town's activity reaches a feverish pitch, all three establishments are sometimes open at the same time.

Next door to the London Inn is St. Neot's famous 13th-century church, which possesses some of the finest stained-glass windows in all of England and thus attracts hundreds of curious photographers and history buffs. It also draws a few dozen parishioners for Sunday services.

The pub, on the other hand, draws about twice that on a typical night, many of whom seek their particular brand of salvation at the bottom of a just-emptied pint glass.

At the London Inn you make friends of all ages, people drawn together by both their geographical intimacy and their love of good beer. And by beer I don't mean the gaseous vapid swill that poses for the noble elixir in our country. No, I mean the creamy grain-scented nectar that the locals drink with nonchalance, the majority of them never having been subjected to the bad stuff. Every quotidian occasion—meeting your mates for a game of skittles, finishing a day of work, completing a round of golf—calls for a pint or two. It is a custom, I must confess, I grew quite fond of. By the end of my stay in St. Neot, I'd sampled nearly 30 different kinds of real English ale, as well as a few stray Irish pints. The proprietor of the London Inn always serves at least six beers on draught (during semi-annual "beer-festival" weeks, that number quintuples) and, I trust, he keeps them at room temperature awaiting your imminent arrival.

Lest I convey the impression that a week of holiday-making in Cornwall is solely about malts and hops, allow me to direct you out the door of the London Inn and onto the peculiar network of mazes that pass as roads in these parts. Narrower than the fairways at the U.S. Open and curvier than doglegs at Augusta, these country lanes are framed on both sides by bountiful hedges, which conceal the granite walls beneath them. If you intend on getting where you want to go in something resembling one piece, I would suggest leaving the driving to someone with at least five years of Cornish navigating experience.

Let him take you to St. Enodoc, a 107-year-old patrician golf club set on dramatic bluffs overlooking the Camel estuary. The course, laid out by the prolific James Braid, has a reputation as the best in Cornwall—and the members seem to know it. Do not come to St. Enodoc, as I did, without a handicap certificate proving your qualifications (24 and lower for men, 30 for women), or you'll encounter a rather stern lady at the reception desk who will scold, frown, and harumph at you in the style of an escaped character from *Fawlty Towers*. It's perhaps the first time I have heard adult men referred to as "naughty boys."

The formality is worth it. St. Enodoc is one of those classic links that make you wonder why you live in a land filled with real-estate-development golf courses: monster sand dunes, including what is probably the world's tallest sand trap, the "Himalaya Bunker" on the sixth hole; endless ocean vistas, like the one from the ninth tee, which constantly delineate the difference between Cornish golf and, say, the Florida variety; ancient hedgerows and stone walls, like the one blithely cutting across the middle of the third hole; and flocks of sheep standing beside the fairways, watching all the comedy from a safe distance. This is a magnificent setting for golf.

But try to hire a caddie. St. Enodoc is filled with blind and semi-blind shots, where you aim toward a marker post and hope. Since there's hardly a flat spot to be found on the entire links, there's often no telling where your ball may end up. Which is the condition some of us face anyway each time we commence to swing.

Depending on how the wind blows—and it always blows in one direction or another—St. Enodoc can play like four different golf courses. All of them, I'm happy to report, eventually lead you to the bucolic 12th green, beside which John Betjeman, the former poet laureate, is buried. He was long a member of the club and sang its praises in verse:

> *He loved each corner of the links—*
> *The stream at the eleventh,*
> *The grey-green bents, the pale sea-pinks,*
> *The prospect from the seventh.*

I suspect anyone with a touch of the poet in his heart might feel the urge to compose a stanza or two of his own after visiting this singular place.

Down one of those inscrutable Cornish roads is Bowood Park, a newish layout built on a rolling 230-acre parcel of farmland. It has much to commend it: good greens, lovely views of the Cornish countryside, and just enough trees to make wayward shots an adventure. Unlike other Cornish links, like the seaside courses Parranporth and Bude, the character of this place is distinctly park-like, a type of golf course that America surely does better than anywhere. If not for the surrounding fields of flax—shimmering lakes of vegetal blue—and the sound of magpies blending with the musical voices of heavily accented locals, you might forget you were in Cornwall at all. Indeed, the presence of some very large, very new homes beside otherwise pristine fairways (with more potential homesites waiting for holiday makers to build upon) bodes ill for Bowood.

Lanhydrock, on the other hand, is a classic parkland course, boasting lots of trees and burns and marauding ditches, all of which come into play with devilish frequency. The course is what the Brits call "sporty." It's short—only

6,200 yards from the back tees—but with enough smartly designed hazards (and gale-force winds) to make it a superb challenge. Do not, however, allow yourself to be conned into a match with a gentleman who passes himself off as the chairman of Lanhydrock's handicap committee, and whose 18 handicap, he will tell you, is therefore beyond reproach—unless you wish to pay this cheerful charlatan's bar tab.

A few minutes down the road from the Lanhydrock golf course is the famed Victorian mansion of the same name. Formerly owned by religious orders, royals, and rich robber barons, it's been restored and maintained by the National Trust, which encourages visitors to tour the home's 49 rooms. Doing so with even a modicum of attentive reflection requires a two-hour journey at least. Now, to hardcore golfers, this might seem like a terrible sacrifice—in the British Isles, after all, two hours is almost enough time to play an entire round of golf—but do it anyway. A jaunt through this perfectly glorious property—part museum, part monument to the Merchant-Ivory school of ineffable loveliness—will tell you more about the English class system than any shrill tract Frederick Engels ever penned.

And it will make your non-playing companion insanely happy.

As will a visit to one of Cornwall's many snapshot-inspiring fishing villages, which attract point-and-shoot holiday makers (including me) seemingly hell-bent on single-handedly doubling the stock prices of Kodak and Fuji. These places, like the painfully cute Palpierro, are so preposterously pretty that you can almost convince yourself that spending an afternoon in one of these tiny mirages, quaffing ale and snacking on vinegar-and-salt-soaked fish and chips, is actually a salutary pursuit.

Golf, we know, is definitely good for you—except when you're something less than a professional golfer attempting to play the back tees on an early Jack Nicklaus course. Then the game can become an exercise in self-flagellation. Yes, Cornwall has its requisite Nicklaus beauty—this one's called St. Mellion, and it was Jack's first design in the British Isles—

154

and, yes, you *will* play it. Why? Because it was several times the host of the Benson & Hedges International, because it's imposing and hard and majestic, and, primarily, because we golfers refuse to run from a golf course just because it's penal, slightly unfair, and way too hard for mere mortals.

No matter where you travel, Jack is like Coca-Cola: omnipresent and inescapable. This Cornish effort is fairly typical early-style Jack, with plenty of deep bunkers and rough, bulldozed mounds framing the fairways, and red, yellow, and white stakes everywhere you look. At St. Mellion, a herd of cows wanders behind the 13th green and a brilliant field of yellow rapeseed fills the horizon, all of which scream *England!* Still, you'll often feel right at home. In the style of American "championship" layouts, the course is grand, an epic track that invites epic shots. But if you cannot author such heroic results, Jack's Cornish debut will surely uncover your inadequacies and hurt your golf feelings, sending you scurrying back to the pub for some kind words and reassuring nourishment.

St. Mellion is also home to a full-service spa, the only one of its kind in the area, where you can enjoy massages and facials and various forms of hydro-therapy that do not involve alcohol.

If you're going to take the waters in Cornwall, though, I suggest bringing a fly rod. This is prime trout territory, and Mr. Jones, the London Inn proprietor, happens to have a couple of secret spots reserved for dedicated anglers. The rewards are great, but the novice should beware: Trout fishing with a fly can be just as frustrating as golf—and possibly as addicting.

As tranquil as an afternoon spent casting your line onto a silent pond may be, nothing in Cornwall, I suggest, will be as good for the golfer's soul as a round at Trevose, a links course laid out by Harry Colt (of Pine Valley fame) beside blustery Constantine Bay. You approach the first tee, mere steps from the office of head professional Gary Aliss, son of ABC commentator Peter, and survey all that awaits you: the ocean, the dunes, and 18 emerald sanctuaries tucked into the rugged brown landscape. And you know you've arrived at a special place.

Trevose is the kind of unmistakably British links where the wind blows so hard at your back that a 460-yard par-4 becomes an easy drive and an 8-iron. Where a 412-yarder the other way becomes unreachable in regulation. Where you play the first two holes swaddled in sweaters and rain gear, and the next 16 in your shirt sleeves. Where public roads, transporting cyclists and dog walkers and ladies on their errands, intersect the golf course. Where a sign reminds members that "four hours is too long for a round of golf." Where the surf crashes against the shore behind the fourth green. Where a good glass of ale and an inquisitive gang of locals awaits you in the clubhouse. Where everything you love about golf is collected in one magical place.

A time of peace and happiness, indeed.

22

THE CANTERBURY
(GOLF) TALES

The county of Kent, hard by the English Channel in the southeast of England, is a land of emerald hills and white cliffs and stark plains exposed to the windy salt air. It is a land ideally suited to links-style golf.

It's also a land of history and drama and intrigue, where kings and archbishops and pirates fought during centuries past for land and honor and plunder. Kent is home to Deal, Sandwich, and countless other of the most aged settlements in Britain, where the narrow cobblestone streets and burnished wooden crossbeams are hundreds of years older than Independence Hall. Above all, this is the land of Chaucer, the immortal 14th-century poet whose *Canterbury Tales* we were all made to suffer through in high-school literature classes, between *Beowulf* and *Paradise Lost*. Indeed, this part of England is home to the magnificent Canterbury Cathedral, the hallowed destination of Chaucer's pilgrims and an edifice so grand and powerful that it could make a true believer out of the most earnest agnostic.

There's a golf course nearby, the Canterbury Golf Club, an idyllic parkland layout on the outskirts of town that seasoned golf travelers will probably find pleasant but unremarkable. It's not championship stuff, but the Canterbury Golf Club is a friendly, gentle place to play golf, and it offers a kind introduction to the region before the intrepid pilgrim takes on the harsh, vexing courses beside the coast.

That is what I was intending to do myself on a recent pilgrimage to the southeast of England—play a little golf, do some sight-seeing, head out for the Channel. But after a round at Canterbury Golf Club, I made a startling discovery.

While I was sipping a warm pint of amber ale in a gloomy pub not more than a solid 3-wood from the towering turrets of Canterbury Cathedral, an elderly gentleman appeared at my side, like a cipher.

He looked ancient, but his eyes were timeless. I couldn't tell if he was 700 years old or born yesterday.

"Goode day to ye, syr," he said in an accent that was unfamiliar to my ears, yet easily deciphered. It was English, but of a dialect I had never heard. "I have been taylynge behind ye, syr, on this fayre daye. And I know your mynd is on this day filled with the wordes of Master Geoffrey Chaucer's lyves. The tailles, they are called."

Before I could respond, he handed me a package, bound in weathered sheep hide and tied with a knotted length of hemp. "Ye will fynde these pleasante onough." I looked at the package—a sheath of papers—and when I looked up again, he was gone.

Now, I confess, the ale was not my first of the afternoon. Still, I was stunned to read the inscription upon the first page: "The Golfe Players' Tailles by Old Tom Chaucer, 1998."

I tried to make sense of the man and his package; I tried to find a reasonable explanation for this moment of magic. But I soon realized the treasure I had been given was like the perfect golf swing, a mystery that we mortals shall never unravel. So allow me, gentle reader, to translate into our modern idiom Old Tom's "tailles" of golf from the land of Chaucer. Like the originals, they are by turns entertaining and educational, bawdy and sober, clever and absurd. I don't know where they came from. But I know I'm glad I found them.

THE DUFFER'S TALE

David had all the latest and best golf equipment. His slacks and shirt (made by a famous manufacturer) were impeccably pressed. And his golf bag bore the name tags of many of the world's most desirable golf courses. David had it all.

All except a golf swing.

One look at him with a club in his hands and you could tell that David was a duffer. His swing was not so much "homemade," like a Lee Trevino or Jim Furyk, as it was patched together, like a jalopy constructed from junkyard refuse. This little deficiency did not, of course, stop David the Duffer from playing the hardest, the most punishing, golf courses on the planet. Armed with a credit card and an undying love of the game, David played every links that would have him.

One fine summer's morning not long ago, David checked into the Royal Hotel in the seaside town of Deal. For hundreds of years the hotel has sat beside the English Channel, welcoming historic luminaries, including Admiral Lord Nelson, Queen Victoria, and Winston Churchill, as well as legions of visiting golfers. As David unpacked his bags, admiring his view of the water and Deal's seaside promenade, he noticed a quaint embroidery hanging on his bedroom wall. It said, "Fear not, dear friend. Fear not."

"Cute," he said to himself, dismissing the embroidery as a mere decoration. But the words would not leave him.

"Fear not?" he thought. "What do I have to fear?"

Indeed, what? Here he was in England, beside the sea, about to play golf at Royal Cinque Ports Golf Club—known to locals simply as "Deal"—a spectacular links course that has played host to dozens of national championships over the years. Known for the fierce wind and dramatic sand dunes that affect nearly every hole of this mighty layout, Royal Cinque Ports is the kind of primal golf course American players long to visit. And here David was, less than an hour from the first tee.

On the short journey to the golf course from the Royal Hotel, David, driving his rental car and dreaming of birdie putts, nearly caused a head-on collision by traveling on the wrong side of the road. For a brief moment he was scared.

"So is that fear?" he wondered aloud.

At Royal Cinque Ports, the young man in the pro shop seemed to have no record of David's reservation. For a moment David was, again, afraid he might miss out on his chance of a lifetime to play these storied links. "Oh, here we are," the young pro said, fishing a slip of paper out from under a stack of memoranda. "Sorry, sir," he said to David. "You're all set to go."

David stood on the first tee of Royal Cinque Ports. The wind, howling in his ears, made the green, only 346 yards in the distance, look a mile away. His first two attempts at an opening drive flew approximately 100 yards forward and 100 yards to the right in a graceful 90-degree curve. Both balls ended up well out of bounds, in the car park. For a moment, David the Duffer was fearful he had damaged a member's automobile. But a kind old man, with a grin on his face and a tartan cap on his pate, waved to David and held up the two wayward balls. Then he placed them side by side back on the golf course—and David's worries quickly passed.

"What is fear?" David asked himself, polishing the face on his new titanium driver. "I surely do not know."

The par-5 fifth hole was straight downwind and David supposed he might be able to reach the green, 491 yards away, in two heroic shots. But his drive found waist-high fescue on the left. And his second found shoulder-high gorse on the right. Both balls, he discovered, were hopelessly lost.

This chain of events occurred with depressing regularity. On the sixth, a short dogleg-right par-4 with a blind approach, David missed the fairway and lost his ball. On the eighth, a gorgeous 163-yard par-3 beside the sea, David got his ball up into the air, where the wind took it to a place he never dreamed possible. This was another ball gone. Likewise on the ninth, a superb par-4 of 400 yards fringed along the fairway with deep steep-faced bunkers, David missed the short grass and sacrificed another ball to the Royal Cinque Ports rough.

When David the Duffer made the turn for home, his affairs became even worse. Because he was playing dead into the wind, the back nine of Royal Cinque Ports exposed David's weaknesses with startling efficiency. And by the time he reached the par-3 14th, a 214-yard brute that was unreachable even with an oversized driver, David was down to his last golf ball.

Having come all the way to Kent to play golf on these hallowed grounds, he did not want to have to walk off the links, missing the closing five holes because he was bereft of balls. One errant shot, one stroke even a few yards off the fairway, and his round at Royal Cinque Ports would come to a premature finish.

David looked into his bag, perusing the shiny instruments of torture he had at his disposal. The ads for his clubs had promised "incredible distance" and "deadly accuracy," but now, exposed to the elements beside the English Channel, they could offer him no solace. The 3-wood? No way. The 4-iron? Forget it; he hadn't hit it straight all day. The 7-iron? The word "shank" came to mind. David fingered the ball in his hand nervously, staring at his clubs. Shaking his head disconsolately, he reached for his putter.

He played from tee to green with the putter on that par-3. And on the 413-yard 15th, and the 469-yard 16th, and the 17th as well. And the 18th, too.

When he reached the final green—after 11 superb putts to the heart of the short grass—David saw a familiar face.

"How was your round, sir?" the kind old man asked David, tipping his tartan cap.

The duffer replied, "Very educational. I played the last five holes at Royal Cinque Ports with one ball. Now," he said, placing his putter back in the bag, "I know what fear means."

161

THE PROFESSIONAL'S TALE

He was quite good, this professional, and he didn't try to pretend otherwise.

"Two questions," he said to the starter at Littlestone Golf Club. "Where's the first tee? And what's the course record?" As the pro strode out of the clubhouse, a long-time member who had overheard the brash visitor's words said to his playing partner, "A cheeky one, that. Strutting around here like a proud cock. A regular Chanticleer, he is."

The pro had heard about this Littlestone golf course— it was consistently ranked in the top 100 in Great Britain— and was eager to test his game on a links whose design had been improved over the years by two gentlemen named James Braid and Alister MacKenzie, who, it was said, knew a bit about landscape architecture. The pro intended to someday play in the British Open Championship, and Littlestone, he knew, was often used as a final qualifying site.

He surveyed the first hole: downwind, straight-away par-4, with two bunkers on either side of the green mouth. Only 297 yards. Easy. The pro selected a 3-wood and took a few elegant and perfectly efficient practice swings. He was ready to show the curious members looking out the clubhouse window what a trained killer could accomplish on a course like Littlestone, a links that played to only 6,470 yards from the tips.

He crushed his tee shot, sending the ball whistling toward the pin. The pro's shiny white pellet landed on the front edge of the green—and shot forward like a bullet out of a gun, running past the hole and through the putting surface over a mound and into a patch of grass so thick that a lawnmower would be frightened of it. The pro spent four more strokes to get down from there and took a bogey on the shortest par-4 he'd seen in 10 years.

By the time he returned to the clubhouse, his face stinging from the salty wind, the pro had swung thrice to reach the green at the 393-yard 12th and twice to reach the green on the 179-yard 17th, as well as three putts on the 18th green, an exhibition the members gleefully witnessed from the lounge overlooking the last.

As the pro trudged off the Littlestone links, he turned back one last time to survey the land he had just navigated. And he laughed.

He laughed long and hard, recalling the 340-yard drive he'd hit with the wind at the fifth, the head-high bunker he had found on the short ninth, and the majestic, 135-yard 2-iron he had hit against the wind on the 16th.

He laughed. For he had shot a 91. And he was certain he had just played the best round of his life.

THE GOLF WIDOW'S TALE

All her husband wanted to do was play golf. The man was a fanatic. Every day during their trip to Kent, the daft man bolted down his breakfast and dashed off to one golf course or another, leaving the Golf Widow behind, alone for the day, until he returned at sundown. As long as the man could find some grassy dunes with 18 holes dug into them, he was insanely happy.

After several days of his antics, the Golf Widow could bear the monotony no more. "Let's do some sight-seeing," she suggested. "Something other than golf!"

"But, Honey," he replied, wondering how his fellow pilgrim could have so suddenly become a heretic, "I'm playing Prince's Golf Club today!"

"So?" she inquired innocently.

"The nineteen thirty-two Open, which Gene Sarazen won? The mounds, the wind, the waves pounding on the shore? Bump-and-run shots? Braving the elements?"

The Golf Widow stared blankly.

"Prince's Golf Club!" the man fairly shouted. "One of the great links courses in England!"

"Who's Gene Sarazen?" she asked in reply.

And so, as the man stormed off once more, intent on filling his day with double-bogeys, the Golf Widow set out to find her own diversions.

At first she considered doing a guided walk, since Kent offered more than 300 to choose from. But she had heard something about golf spoiling good walks—or something like that—and opted instead to seek out the most purely "touristy" attractions she could bear. She was, after all, a tourist, the Golf Widow reminded herself, entitled to frivolous pleasures.

The best attractions she found that fateful day were a tour of Dover Castle, where actors re-enacted a medieval siege; a visit to the town of Rochester Upon Medway, known as the "City of Great Expectations" because of the many references made to it by Charles Dickens; and a modern re-creation of the *Canterbury Tales*, performed in—where else?—the town of Canterbury, a few steps from the towering cathedral of Geoffrey Chaucer's poem.

For the sake of frivolity—and also because she just liked the sound of it—the Golf Widow wanted to eat a sandwich in Sandwich. And she did, at a sandwich "bar" named Yummies that offered more than 50 varieties of the venerable meal.

She was free, free of golf. But she wasn't far from it. Even as she explored the English countryside, her man was only a few minutes away, digging up the divots. She felt, if only for an afternoon, she should like to escape, to transport herself away from the game that had turned her mate into a single-minded madman. And that is when she noticed on her road map that she was only 15 minutes from the Channel Tunnel—the "Chunnel"—less than an hour away from France where, she supposed, nobody cared much about British Opens and a man named Sarazen.

"I shall have an afternoon snack in France," she declared, pointing her car toward Folkestone. To her delight, the train to France was designed to accommodate passengers *and* their cars, so she merely drove onboard, reclined the driver's seat, and enjoyed the 35-minute ride. When the train was once again on land, the Golf Widow was in Calais.

As she bit into a warm airy crêpe slathered with chocolate sauce, she realized this was the first time in her life she'd been able to visit England and France in the same day. She realized also that she would be back in Kent in time to join her crazy man for a plate of fish and chips. And for a moment, she thought that crêpe was the most delicious thing she had ever tasted.

THE HUSBAND OF BATH'S TALE

Married five times and still uncertain of how to keep a wife, the Husband of Bath devoted much of his life to playing golf. It was only on the golf course that he felt at peace, where divorces and calamity could be put aside for a few hours and the biggest dilemma in his day was whether to approach the greens with a lofted pitch or a running chip.

But then the Husband of Bath met Tamara, a red-headed bewitcher, and he was flummoxed.

She was the assistant chef at the Wallets Court Hotel, a sublimely peaceful place near Dover, in a tiny village called St. Margaret's-on-Cliff, once home to Noel Coward and Ian Fleming. The Husband of Bath had spent the night at Wallets Court to partake of the comfortable accommodations and, even more so—for he loved to eat!—to sample a meal at the restaurant, which was renowned in Kent for being one of the loveliest in all the county. And that is how he met dear Tamara. As soon as he had one bite of the tender sole she had made for him, the Husband of Bath knew he was in love.

He ardently proclaimed his devotion to the flame-haired beauty, promising her that the five who had come before her were nothing but bad memories. She smiled coyly at him and promised she would be his wife forever, if only he could answer one question.

"Yes, of course!" the Husband agreed.

"And if you cannot, I will never speak to you again," Tamara warned. "My question is one that has tormented men and women alike throughout the ages. It is this: What, I ask you, does every golfer want more than anything in the world?"

The Husband of Bath thought hard, but was not certain of his answer. "I need a day to think about it," he said.

"As you wish," Tamara said. "Do not disappoint me."

The next morning, the Husband of Bath drove up the coast to Sandwich, where he found the Royal St. George's Golf Club, site of numerous British Opens, a brilliant gauntlet that has produced champions ranging from J.H. Taylor (1894) and Walter Hagen (1922) to Greg Norman (1993). As he toured these stellar links, routed through sand dunes that seemed at times three stories high—indeed the fourth has a bunker nearly 30 feet tall—the Husband of Bath mulled Tamara's question. "What does every golfer want? What does every golfer want?" he asked himself.

As the wind blew in gales and the Husband of Bath bounced his ball around Royal St. George's firm fairways, he came to understand the answer to Tamara's riddle. As he stood on the eighth tee, a perfect uphill-downhill par-4 of 410 yards, feeling the wind in his hair and the good earth beneath his feet, seeing rare orchids in the rough and the churning sea beyond the bluffs, the Husband of Bath knew.

"What every golfer wants," he said out loud as he approached his tee shot, "is to play the game of golf upon a course as magical as Royal St. George's."

From nowhere, Tamara appeared at the Husband's side, a golf bag slung over her shoulder.

"Hello, my darling," she said, smiling broadly and kissing her Husband upon his cheek. "May I join you for the back nine?"

23

GOLF IN THE
ARCTIC CIRCLE

Is there anywhere left on this shrinking planet where a hacker cannot find a nicely manicured patch of greenness to tee his ball and let the slices fly? Is there any country on Earth where the intrepid chunkmeister can't find a reasonably maintained golf course on which to dig the sod? All right, some of the less developed stretches of the Amazon, perhaps, and maybe atop each of the polar ice caps. But the fact is, the most unlikely places are no longer immune from the viral spread of worldwide golf fever.

Which leaves the fearless traveler in an enviable predicament: Bring the sticks along, cumbersome as they may be, or risk missing a once-in-a-lifetime chance to shoot a career round in, say, Indonesia. Or Venezuela. Or Finland.

Golf in Finland? Parts of which reside above the Arctic Circle? Where reindeer outnumber those who have heard of a funny old place in Scotland called St. Andrews? Finland, whose Lapland tundra would seem to befit a good old-fashioned NFC playoff game, not lob-wedge flop shots? Finland, the Land of Ice, where you think Sibelius, not Seve Ballesteros? That Finland?

The easternmost of the Scandinavian countries is best known in America for its distance runners, orchestral conductors, and, in the case of native-son Renny Harlin, directors of expensive and unwatchable action movies. Still, Finland has 89 golf courses and something like 50,000 registered players. Although that last figure is roughly equivalent to the number of people waiting for a tee time at your local American muni course on a Saturday afternoon, the first figure should help you gauge how golf crazy this country has become. Especially since you can play here only about six months a year.

When you *can* play, however, you can often do so without ever stopping for the usual obstacles that vex hackers back home—for instance, nightfall. Even at its southernmost, Finland is situated above the 60th parallel, so it's possible in the heart of summer to play 72 holes (or more) in one day, beginning, if you like, at midnight. With enough caffeine—and an extra sleeve or two of balls—you could conceivably play an uninterrupted two-month-long game here. Which, no doubt, some golf-obsessed Finn, well-fortified with the local lingonberry liqueur, is planning to do as soon as the permafrost encasing his in-ground sauna starts to melt.

An excellent place to start such an odyssey would be in Helsinki, where more than 20 courses are within an hour of the airport. Nearly all the golf courses around Helsinki are supposed to be good, primarily because the city is blessed with one of Finland's best natural resources: lots of wide-open spaces. I can confidently recommend two tracks, which I visited (and wreaked considerable havoc upon) not long ago. Aside from Sarfvik Golf Club, which is said to be the most exclusive (and lovely) of Finnish country clubs, the hottest ticket in the Baltic region is the Helsinki Golf Club, the oldest course in the country. That said, do not expect a centuries-old weather-beaten Temple of the Game, where Old Tom Morris stalked the fairways and James Braid worked his architectural magic. Remember, this is *Finland*. Helsinki Golf Club opened in 1932.

It was then, rumor has it, that two young reindeer herders, Paarvi Tuulvitskoog and Olaaferinn "Ollie" Ruukinaanaluu, were batting around a frozen herring with a finely polished reindeer antler, seeing which lad could slide the slippery kipper into a far-off vodka bottle—a recently emptied one—with the fewest whacks of the horn. They called their game *paar en fisken* ("hit the fish"), or "paar" for short. When the boys learned that the Scots had come up with a similar game many years previous, they immediately sold their animals and moved to Glasgow. But "paar," or golf, as it soon became known, was to be forever entrenched in the Finnish sports consciousness.

Though this fable may or may not be true, it does illustrate several important concepts about golf in Finland. The first is, if you play here, don't bother bringing your "A" game. You'll need at least a "double A" version. The second is that reindeer really do wander the land and you should take care not to damage their exquisite racks with wayward drives.

Helsinki Golf Club is neither particularly elegant nor awe-inspiring, merely delightful. The course has all the hallmarks of classical design: smartly constructed green complexes that leave plenty of room for imaginative running shots; tee boxes situated a short sensible walk from the previous hole; and much of the land left as it was found. The second, for instance, a 378-yard par-4, works gently uphill over rugged terrain that has never seen a bulldozer, bending around a grove of stolid trees. This hole's green, on a small plateau, sits near a red barn and feels remarkably solitary and peaceful.

Helsinki Golf Club's parcel of turf, a serene tree-filled park in the heart of the city, makes a game here seem like a pleasing walk through a metropolitan oasis. If, however, the wind picks up—as it did when I was there—all your "walk-in-the-park" reveries will be literally blown away: the place can feel like a seaside links in the heart of monsoon season. I hit one pop-up drive, from the elevated 10th tee, that threatened for a few horrifying moments to land behind me. If you're greeted with such conditions, fear not: A hot bowl of Finnish sausage soup awaits in the clubhouse.

Across town, at Master Golf, you don't need to have

won a PGA Tour event to receive an invitation. But being an American does help: This pretty 27-hole complex, set in a pristine kettle surrounded by a rugged moraine, is about as close an approximation to a States-style layout you'll find in Finland. Indeed, this was one of only two courses I saw in the entire country where someone dared to ride a golf buggy. (To be fair, he might have been suffering from lingonberry hangover.) If the weather were about 20 degrees warmer and they put up a few T-shirt shacks and calabash seafood joints, you might swear you were playing in Myrtle Beach.

The first hole has an island green buttressed by railroad ties, and at least nine others feature man-made lakes and ponds that require either heroic carries or very straight tee shots. Many of the green complexes, such as the one at the par-3 sixth, a pretty little hole that looks transplanted from Palm Springs, are finely manicured, with sharply cut fringes and collars. Master Golf is one of the newer courses in Finland and has all the modern amenities. Which is to say you'll alternately hear the elegiac chirp of jays in the plentiful white birches and the electronic chirp of Finnish cell phones ringing. Golf may just be catching on here, but wireless technology is already a runaway sensation. (Nokia, the cell phone giant, is headquartered in Finland.) In fact, the Finns may be the most cellular people on the planet. It's not unusual to be in a fine Helsinki restaurant and look up from your plate of smoked reindeer tongue to see three of the party of four across the aisle chattering on their miniature walkie-talkies.

To get the *au naturel* golf-in-the-Finnish-wilds experience, you need to travel north a bit—like to Lapland, near the Arctic Circle. There you'll find two most peculiar golf courses, places whose exotica quotient is nearly off the scale. The first is called Arctic Golf Club, which you may deduce if you haven't been sipping too much of the lingonberry elixir, is situated on the Arctic Circle. The course's name may seem at first blush a raving oxymoron, but I assure you this is no hoax. It's *green* here during the summer.

People wear collared shirts and rayon slacks, not animal hides. Golf can be—and is—played.

Actually, the course is terrific, a dramatic smartly designed layout that takes advantage of the region's topographical beauty. Towering trees are the main obstacle here, and Sahalee-like, they guard many of the fairways and greens. The 18th, a downhill par-3, cuts through a swath of virgin forest. Hit an errant tee ball and you might as well add a penalty stroke to your scorecard. So verdant, so remarkably plush is the Arctic Golf Club, you have to remind yourself that only a few months after you've chunked out your last divot, they'll be playing "winter rules" here, with snowshoes and orange balls. About the only clue that you're a long way from the equator is the frequent appearance of a local fellow who likes to play his golf dressed as Santa Claus. (How he makes a full shoulder turn wearing that big red coat is beyond me—though the Laplanders say it might have something to do with the medicinal properties of the magical lingonberry.)

A bit farther to the balmy south and cosmopolitan west, you'll find the Green Zone Golf Club, which sits on the Finnish-Swedish border. Literally. About half the holes are in Finland, and the other half are in the Land of Parnevik. (The clubhouse attendants will be happy to provide you with a stamped customs form before you—and your flying golf balls—start crossing international boundaries.) In the case of the sixth, a short par-3 with water long and left, you tee off in one country (Finland) and putt out in another (Sweden). Since these neighboring nations observe different time zones, the metaphysical ramifications of making a hole-in-one here—*Did it really happen in the present?*—would befuddle Kierkegaard, even if he does have a double "a" in his name.

After a round at the Green Zone, consider indulging in that admirable Finnish tradition known as the sauna bath. Unlike our tepid American version, the Finnish sauna experience includes not only the usual smoldering rocks, but also a soapy sponge bath administered by a Teutonic female attendant—"Now you vill roll over!"—and plenty of cold beer. (In the sauna.) It's a lovely way to rid the arctic from your bones.

Before departing this part of the world, don't miss the chance to play golf 20 minutes across the Gulf of Finland, in Tallinn, Estonia. (There are all sorts of regularly scheduled flights from Helsinki, but the most memorable is in a vintage DC-3 that never rises above 7,000 feet.) Liberated from Soviet oppression, this independent Baltic state is flexing its recently discovered free-market muscles, like a foal trotting for the first time. The locals will be awfully glad to have you, and to listen incredulously when you tell them that back in America we have thousands, tens of thousands, of places to play golf.

The golf course in Tallinn is called Niitvalja. Built amid a majestic birch forest, it's the first—and thus far, only—golf course in the entire country. And it's a good one, reminiscent of the North Carolina sand hills, minus the pines. When you play the only golf course in Estonia, you have an odds-on chance of getting paired with a member of the National Team. And if you're really lucky, you might get to duff it around with a 17-year-old with a 5-handicap who has never broken par.

He's the Estonian National Champion.

24

LE GOLF

There are four pernicious myths about France I would like to promptly dispel:

1) *Jerry Lewis.* After extensive research into the matter, I have yet to meet a French person who finds his zany movies the pinnacle of cinematic genius, comic or otherwise.

2) *Mickey Rourke.* Ditto.

3) *The French are rude and arrogant, especially if you don't speak their highly refined and beautiful language.* Non! C'est absurde. C'est une idée bizarre. Quel idiot!

4) *There ain't no golf in these here parts.* Sure—and there's nothing good to drink, either.

Actually, not only will you find good golf in France, you'll occasionally find *great* golf, the quality of which, were it in the British Isles, would inspire breathless cover stories and top 100 commendations from the putatively reputable golf magazines, whose business it is to alert their readers to the Next Big Destination. Alas, this is France, land of wine and cheese and absurdly gorgeous architecture. You're not supposed to find glorious golf courses here. You're supposed to be too busy visiting the Eiffel Tower and the Louvre. Repeat after the various national tourism promotion councils: *France is not a golf destination. France is not …*

News flash: Recently I spent two weeks puttering through the French countryside, getting lost on impossibly charming rural roads, stopping for *une baguette* and *un verre*—okay, *une bouteille—de vin*, playing golf on the grounds of a majestic château, dining later at a glorious temple of gastronomy, sleeping (with a very good-looking lady) in an ancient manor house, and doing the whole thing again the next day.

I ask you, does life get any sweeter? If so, please send instructions in care of this publisher.

The French Riviera and parts of Bordeaux have several world-class golf courses. But there are also several delightful golf courses in and around Paris, which, for someone conditioned to believe that every square foot of the world's most beautiful city is covered with museums, boutiques, and crêpe stands, comes as a revelation, if not a Gallic shock. These are not just okay places, either. These are the kind of golf courses you'd be happy to play every day—if only you could conjugate irregular verbs better.

Morfontaine, St. Cloud, and St. Nom-la-Breteche are all fine golf courses, but they normally don't take visitors. Indeed, these tournament-worthy courses embody the kind of elitism and employ the kind of exclusionary tactics one expects from America's snootiest country clubs, not a socialist nation of *égalité*. On the other hand, public facilities, like the 36-hole layout at the Stade Français in Courson, about 40 minutes from the heart of Paris, disarm you with their welcome.

The Courson courses also disorient you a bit, especially if the side effects of the Grand Cru du Bordeaux you and your companion quaffed the previous evening have not quite left you. Block out the chattering in French and the motorized golf carts, and you can imagine you're in the rugged heart of Scotland, not minutes from the cosmopolitan Champs-Elysées. This is fun golf: windy, dry, heavily mounded, and full of locals out for a walk. At Courson you're geographically close to the insufferable rudeness of the clerks at Galeries Lafayette, but the niceness of a day here is countries away in spirit.

You'll find even finer golf close to the city. Take, for instance, St. Germain, an excellent Harry Colt design in the western suburbs, a pleasant 30-minute train ride—and an even shorter drive—from the Arc de Triomphe. This friendly private club welcomes outside play during the week and allows weekend guests when escorted by a member. The place feels much like Gleneagles, thanks to its Scottish-style bunkering and heathery waste areas. But it has a distinctly French feel, too, for St. Germain is situated in a dense forest, with a surfeit of birds and critters and, one supposes, white truffles. The par-3s here are exceptionally lovely and the local players, who bring their spouses with them for walking company, are even lovelier in their politeness and good humor. Golf at St. Germain is terrific; that you have the charms of Paris awaiting you when you're done chasing your ball through the woods makes it even more so.

This concept of golf by day, gourmand by night, is not, I know, a new one, nor even necessarily a unique one. But I also know this: It is a concept that takes a little getting used to. Very little. Like about five seconds. If you love golf and you love food, if you love spending your days outside in the countryside and your nights in impossibly romantic inns, if you love nature and passion and beauty and everything else sublime and joyous about being alive, this inimitably French daily double is about the most magical concept since four-day work weeks and low-fat ice cream.

Consider, for instance, Fontainebleau, a golf course that would burn in your memory even if it weren't minutes from Barbizon, home of countless painters and poets and inebriated journalists. Fontainebleau is not merely a fun place to play golf, a pretty location to work up an appetite for your nightly nine-course two-bottles-of-wine repast. No, Fontainebleau is perfection. If you give any credence to top-10 lists and all that, let me share this: Fontainebleau is easily one of the five best golf courses I have ever played. And it's in *France*, for crissake!

Ancient forest, thrillingly rolling terrain, exciting bunkering—there's not a single bad hole here. There's not a drop of water, either. Not even a wee creek. Just natural magnificence, with plenty of room to play Scottish runners into the greens. Speaking of which, some of the putting surfaces at Fontainebleau are severe enough to inspire the dreaded 4-putt (I have empirical evidence), but constructed well enough to accept all manner of well-played approaches. Fontainebleau is a special golf course.

It alone is worth the 90-minute trip south from Paris. But the Fontainebleau experience is made doubly superb by spending an evening in Barbizon at the Bas-Breau, which takes the phrase "charming country hotel" to ridiculously new heights. The Bas-Breau is a member of Relais & Chateaux, an association of extraordinary upscale hotels and restaurants around the world, founded in France. The original inductees into Relais & Chateaux were a series of inns linking Paris with Lyon to the south. The traveler fortunate enough to stay in these impeccable hotels was said to have journeyed on "the happiness road."

After nearly two weeks of staying in places like the Bas-Breau, elegant and tasteful places that look like they've been conceived by the production designer for *Howard's End*, I'm inclined to amend the nickname of the Relais & Chateaux route to "the drunk, giddy, and preposterously well-fed road." But that's probably too long for their brochures.

A delightful way to see the golf courses of France (and the hotels and restaurants at night) is to rent a car in Paris and drive yourself through tiny storybook villages, with their narrow cobblestone streets and ancient buildings. This method is not only *très romantique*, but it allows you the flexibility to delay or—perish the thought—*cancel* a round of golf in case the phrase *"plus de vin rouge, s'il vous plaît"* sprang from your lips too many times the night before.

One of my favorite golf-gourmand daily doubles can be found in Joigny, a relatively big town (about 10,000 people) in the heart of Burgundy, near Chablis. Joigny, as students of the *Guide Michelin* will tell you, is the famous home of La Côte St. Jacques, a rare three-star apotheosis of dining run by superstar chef Michel Lorain and his dashing son Jean-Michel. At the nearby Golf du Roncemay, when I told one of the nice Frenchmen with whom I was playing that I was staying at Lorain's place, my fellow golfer set down his club and said solemnly, "Ah, Lorain! He is a great cooker!"

Lorain *fils* is also a devoted golfer. Thus, he and his family have renovated the Roncemay course, a roughly hewn rolling layout set in a towering oak forest completely removed from civilization, save for the highly civilized wine cellar maintained at the clubhouse dining room. Given its proximity to virtually nothing but grazing land, Roncemay is often startlingly empty—and eager for guests. The place is very friendly, very beautiful, and very challenging. But, to be frank, it's merely an appetizer for what the hungry golfer may look forward to in the evening. In a word: *Lorain*.

Golf in the morning, romance in the afternoon, sea scallops in a cappucino broth (seriously!) at night, a bottle of *premier cru* Chablis to send you off to bed—days like these make you profoundly grateful to be alive and in France.

The only danger in this high life may be a heightened exposure to alcohol poisoning and the slight risk of contracting a mild case of three-star-restaurants-every-night gout. Otherwise, we're talking eternal bliss. Even getting from one golf course to another is a pleasure. Driving through the Burgundian countryside, a phalanx of emerald checkerboards dotted with fields of yellow rapeseed and snowy white cows, you pass through the center of medieval villages, postcard hamlets with stone roads barely wide enough to fit a compact Renault. Each of these towns has just the vital accouterments: a *boulangerie-pâtisserie*; a post office; and, perhaps most important, a *fromagerie*, where you can purchase pungent chunks of local goat cheese that is strong enough to stop an elephant in its tracks, but subtle enough to inspire celebratory sonnets. These tiny French towns are so pretty you want to cry.

Alas, there is golf to be played. Scenic golf. Golf in the shadow of a centuries-old château.

Château de Chailly is such a golf course. It's the kind of

layout a seasoned hacker might dismiss as unremarkable—were it not situated at the foot of a 500-year-old castle. It's the kind of golf course you might call a "cow patch"—until you realize that up until five years ago it *was* a cow patch. A low stone fortress wall comes into play on two of the holes, and there are just enough bunkers to make approach shots interesting. But the main appeal of Chailly is this: Every time you look up from a par putt, you see the majestic château and the even more majestic countryside looming before you.

What's more, only a few miles from the golf course is one of the great restaurants on Earth, Bernard Loiseau's La Côte d'Or, or, as the cognoscenti simply call it, Loiseau. Forgive me for harping on this daily-double theme, but that's the way it is with certain truths: They make themselves so insistently apparent you cannot ignore them. And you must repeat them. Our man Loiseau was the subject of an American book called *Burgundy Stars*, which chronicled the campaign of a provincial Burgundian chef to get his restaurant upgraded from two to three stars by the career-making *Guide Michelin*. I'll spare you the suspense: He was successful. And an evening spent at Loiseau's spectacular hotel and restaurant in the village of Saulieu is one you'll always remember fondly, no matter how many bogeys you made at Château de Chailly.

Assuming you've survived your trip along the happiness road, pausing at exceedingly happy establishments like the Auberge les Templiers, where I had the single most delicious course of the hundreds of courses I feasted on in France (a grilled slice of foie gras soaked in a sweet sauce of tangerines and celery roots), a special treat awaits you. That is, if you can still button your golf pants.

The place is called Les Bordes, built by the late Baron Bich (of pen and razor renown). It's a country retreat in the Loire Valley, close to Sancerre and Pouilly, dangerously so for those trying vainly to stay on the wagon. Depending on your priorities, you may view this manicured playground as either a particularly good golf course or a remarkably good bird sanctuary or both. The layout, designed by the American architect Robert Von Hagge, may be the best conditioned in France, meandering through woodlands and marshes and meadows, providing a stern but utterly enjoyable test. And even if the golf weren't so aesthetically pleasing, so good—the course is regularly rated the best in the country by the authoritative *Peugeot Golf Guide*—the serenade (and sight) of brilliant yellow finches and wild pheasant and, unbelievably to an American from Los Angeles, cuckoos, makes a day spent at Les Bordes an experience to be cherished.

Soon after you check into the lovely on-site hotel overlooking the 18th fairway, you'll likely meet the man who helped construct this impeccable golf course, an American fellow named Jim Shirley, who looks after the course. He'll know you've arrived because he'll see the Stars & Stripes the staff flies in your honor, as they do with the national flag of every foreign guest. Jim Shirley is about the nicest man you could know, and he loves to talk golf over a good bottle of St. Emillion. (And who doesn't?)

Before you depart Les Bordes, before you say goodbye to the unspoiled countryside and return to Paris, note the Rodin statue overlooking the practice putting green. Note the 12th-century cross adjacent to the sixth hole, the helipad behind the 12th hole (for when guys like Clint Eastwood decide to pop in after the Cannes Film Festival), the white swan guarding the 17th tee, the startling quiet descended over the land like a shroud of mist, the heathery purple wild flowers growing in the rough, the deer peeking through the woods, the aching beauty that one can never quite reprise—note it all. And be glad you are in France.

25

EL GOLF

The Spanish know how to enjoy life.

Green olives soaked in lime juice; late-afternoon siestas filled with rest and romance; Jose Carreras singing Catalan folk songs; breaded *boquerones*—little finger-sized fish—eaten whole, like so many french fries; the flamenco, danced to a trio of plaintive guitars; thin cool glasses of manzanilla; dinner, with plenty of fresh seafood and a good bottle of Rioja, at 10 PM; dancing until dawn; beauty everywhere you look.

And golf.

If the game doesn't immediately strike you as one of life's sensual pleasures—in the same vein as green olives and the voice of Carreras—you haven't played in Spain. For Americans conditioned to think of golf as a kind of penury, a four-hour test to be endured, the concept of golf as a hedonistic treat might seem, well, *foreign*. There's a lightness here, a love of the land and the sun and the air, a happiness. Golf in Spain is, like so much else in this country, about enjoyment.

Go. Enjoy.

If you remember the 1997 Ryder Cup, you know that golf in Spain is not merely a passing fad, the latest way to bring in well-capitalized tourists. The golf courses were here before Tiger and Company arrived, and they'll be here waiting for you—and every other passionate golfer on the planet—for many pleasurable years to come. It's amusing to think of a young Seve Ballesteros working on his short game on the streets of Madrid or Jose Maria Olazabal practicing sand shots in the middle of a provincial bullring. But the truth is that a nation doesn't produce champions like Seve Ballesteros and Jose Maria Olazabal without having some magnificent places to play.

The best of these places would be in Andalucia, the southernmost region of the country, which stretches from the Portuguese border across most of the Iberian peninsula to Málaga. Given the vast geographical sprawl, you'll find a delightful variety of cultures and visions in Andalucia. Moorish castles, endless olive groves, gleaming "white towns" of freshly scrubbed stucco, dusty bodegas suffused with the local sherry—welcome to the land of Cervantes.

This sunny corner of Spain includes the magical city of Seville, birthplace of Hadrian and site of some of the most charming old streets in Europe, narrow rivulets of stone that beg to be walked. Preferably while humming snippets from *Carmen*.

Andalucia is home to coastal resorts like Marbella, a beautiful town filled with beautiful people doing beautiful things with their beautiful toys. Tiptoe through the streets of Puerto Banús, clogged with late-night revelers and Rolls-Royces and other hallmarks of conspicuous consumption and, taking care not to trip over an Arab sheik or a dissipated aristocrat, gawk at the yachts parked in the harbor like so many Toyotas.

In Andalucia you'll also find Jerez, an ancient city best known for pleasures that, depending on how you combine them, may or may not complement each other: flamenco dancing, horses, and sherry. Andalucia was where Columbus embarked for the New World. It was the home of Velazquez, Zurbaran, and Murillo. And where Picasso was born.

This artistic pedigree translates to the golf courses of

the region, which are, almost without exception, aesthetically pleasing. No matter how well or how badly you golf in Andalucia, you'll be delighted to golf in Andalucia. Just look around. Beauty everywhere.

The loveliest golf course of them all is, of course, Valderrama, the Augusta National of Spain. Ranked by some as the top course in all of Europe—the continent, mind you, that includes Scotland, Ireland, Wales, and England among its constituents—Valderrama is one of those Temples of Golf that can make you feel alternately humble and ecstatic. So finely manicured is this layout, so impeccably maintained, I was initially afraid to take a divot. Hit a shot fat here and you feel as though you've gouged a chunk out of the neighbor's living-room carpet.

Cork trees line the fairways and on some holes, notably the second and 13th, they sit *in* the fairways. You must play clever positional golf here—unless, like me, you've never actually seen a cork tree up close and wish to use your round at Valderrama to intimately familiarize yourself with these botanical wonders. (They're pleasingly spongy.) The greens, as you may recall from the Ryder Cup matches, are fast and furious, and opportunities to score some very large numbers abound. In case you're nearing the end of your round and haven't already carded a double-bogey or two, I recommend plunking at least one or two approach irons into the lake fronting the controversial 17th green, just to feel a sense of communion with the noble warriors who likewise drowned their balls in defense of their continent's golfing honor.

You might, with good reason, assume that holy ground like Valderrama is closed to all but the blessed 300 or so members of the club. Incredibly, Valderrama does accept a limited amount of outside play: Between noon and 2 PM, eight tee times are set aside each day for visitors. You merely need to call well in advance, and you'll be welcomed.

Imagine such a policy at Augusta National.

What Valderrama lacks in stuffiness is almost made up for by Royal Sotogrande, just down the road. Opened in

1964—which makes it one of the oldest courses on the Costa del Sol—the highly private Sotogrande has about it a whiff of elitism that, if you're missing snooty American country clubs, will make you feel right at home. In the grand scheme of golf, the sniffy attitude here, which emanates from the sour pro-shop staff like a bad odor, is not unbearable. But in Spain, where you're generally drenched with kindness, it stands out like a plate of mussels that's been left sitting in the sun.

Never mind, though, because a round at Sotogrande is one of the most visually pleasing you'll ever have. The course, a Robert Trent Jones masterpiece, has more of the architect's trademark doglegs than the Humane Society, and they're almost all lined with gorgeous palm, eucalyptus, and, yes, cork trees. Not to mention ponds, lakes, and creeks. This is the kind of golf course you would be happy to play every day of your life: formidably challenging but immensely playable, with a perfect balance between short gems and long monsters. And lots of ravishing flowers and plants and growing things. As I made my way around this stunningly gorgeous layout, all I could do was periodically mumble, "What a treat. What a treat," to nobody in particular.

My eloquence suffered further at Alcaidesa Links, where about all I could muster was, "Wow! Wow!" The source of my awestruck gurglings was the Rock of Gibraltar, which is in plain view from nearly every hole of this charming and decidedly un-Spanish layout, nestled on cliffs overlooking the Mediterranean Sea. I felt about the Rock as I did about the Pyramids of Giza: You know these wonders are extant in the world, and you figure you'll get to see them sometime in your life if you're lucky, but when you actually do see them, you feel surprised, as though you secretly suspected you never really would see them. So go ahead, gawk. Hit your driver to the edge of a cliff facing toward North Africa and gawk. Line up your putt with Gibraltar looming on the horizon and gawk.

The locals say Alcaidesa is the closest thing to a true links course in Spain. I'd say it *is* a true links course: virtually treeless, windy, exposed to the elements, and hard by the sea. Except the winds are warm, the elements are soft, and the sea is substantially calmer than the North Atlantic, amigo. Though its more famous neighbors deservedly garner most of the golf attention in the Sotogrande area, Alcaidesa is a memorable golf course you shouldn't miss.

Situated between Alcaidesa and Valderrama, the San Roque Club is set among the gentle hills of Sotogrande, providing dramatic elevation changes on many of the holes. Speckled with almost as many water hazards as spectacular views, San Roque can be a stern challenge from the back tees, from which aspiring professionals play during the PGA European Tour Qualifying School, held here each November. Unless you're a scratch golfer, I suggest choosing a launching pad slightly closer to the green. Regrettably, many of the German tourists who favor this golf course operate by the "I paid my money, I'm gonna see every inch of this place" ethos. Thus, the pace of play can sometimes be shockingly reminiscent of American standards.

San Roque is not an easy golf course. But it's a reasonable one: Hit decent shots here and you'll score well; hit bad ones and you'll pay the price. As I can attest.

In addition to the fine golf course, San Roque is home to one of the most elegant hotels in the area. Indeed, it's where our boys—and Europe's—rested their weary heads during the Ryder Cup.

As you head west across Andalucia to the fringes of the province of Cadiz, you seem to move incrementally back in time as well. Many of the small towns still carry the appellation *"de la frontera,"* signifying the nebulous frontier between Moors and Christians in days of yore. Carthaginians and Romans and Visigoths all settled in this area. The town of Cadiz itself claims to be the oldest city in the Western world, dating to 1100 B.C.

It's something of a historical collision, then, to find in this ancient land a decidedly young golf course. A precocious golf course. A *modern* golf course. Built next to an international racetrack. By Jack Nicklaus.

It's called Montecastillo, and if you're in Andalucia, you should play it. (For a preview of this superb layout, watch the Golf Channel for the PGA European Tour's Volvo Masters.) Routed through rugged, rolling countryside unspoiled by fairway-choking housing developments—indeed, the only two man-made structures visible from the course are the scoring pylon at the adjacent Jerez Grand Prix circuit and the imposing castle-hotel that swaddles visitors in boundless luxury—Montecastillo is a gentle natural setting for a game of golf. This is something you don't often find yourself saying about Jack's courses, many of which look like they've eschewed the hand of God in favor of the blade of the bulldozer. Here, though, the terrain has been left to do its work, and the results are thrilling.

Early Nicklaus designs are often severe, contrived, and, frankly, not much fun for anyone who doesn't play golf as well as, say, Jack Nicklaus. But Montecastillo, built in 1992, is what you might call "late Jack," the work of a confident architect tempered by experience. This is a softer less edgy Nicklaus golf course. Peacocks roam around the first tee. It's fun. And for $43—only $27 if you stay at the hotel—Montecastillo is a world-class bargain.

And frequently spectacular. The elevated 18th tee, surveying the fairway hundreds of feet below, with a sparkling lake on one side and the castle on the other, is perhaps the most dramatic spot to launch a drive in all of Spain. Just ask Sandy Lyle. During a tournament here not long ago, the former Masters champion reputedly hit his ball into the hotel swimming pool.

❖ ❖ ❖

The province of Huelva, gateway to Portugal, is famous throughout Spain for its ham and amontillado. But to the average Spaniard, Huelva is best known for containing the town of Lepe, an otherwise unremarkable place that serves as the butt of many Spanish jokes—as New Jersey does for Americans. Huelva is also home to several terrific golf courses, two of which, in the spirit of Michelin stars, warrant a special diversion.

The best of the two is Islantilla, a 27-hole complex on the ocean that winds through a densely forested park. Overlooking the Atlantic—the view from the third green is particularly awe-inspiring—Islantilla plays with the windiness of a links course combined with the ball-gobbling testiness of a lushly foliated American layout. It's like a classic James Bond villainess: seductively attractive, but mean as a cornered raccoon. Bring plenty of ammo.

Less than a decade old, the course has hosted European Tour events but is open to the public. And by open, I mean *open*. A weekly pass here costs only $171. Try not to gloat when you think of what your buddies are paying to play six-hour rounds back in the States.

Those of us who live in large cities that have too many residents and too few golf courses harbor a secret fantasy. We see ourselves one day moving to a smaller more sensible town, where one can join a lovely little country club without investing $50,000 or more in initiation fees. Where one can play golf with a trio of friends, in a pretty park filled with songbirds and centuries-old trees.

Okay, maybe it's just my fantasy. But I felt it coming true at Bellavista, a classic, old-styled, country club minutes from the city of Huelva.

This is neither a resort golf course nor a so-called "championship" layout. It's a charming private club (which welcomes outside play) that constantly reminds you golf is not about motorized carts and linoleum-slick greens and 7,200 yards of spirit-breaking misery. Bellavista is, as the name suggests, about nice views and stately trees and friendly companionship. It's about having a charming place to play a game that's often far too charmless.

This is no Valderrama. I didn't leave Bellavista thinking I had just toured one of the greatest golf courses on the planet.

Instead, I thought I would very much like to move to a small village in Spain, near a quaint old golf course, where the monthly dues are about $40 (!), the neighbors are kind, and the local park happens to have 18 holes dug in it.

A place where, after you've put the clubs away, a plate of green olives and a cool glass of manzanilla awaits. Where pleasure abounds. Where you can bask in the sound of Jose Carreras and dance the flamenco deep into the night.

26

JUGADORES
Y PELOTAS

If you're brave enough to take up golf, a funny old game that requires the average player to endure nearly perpetual tribulations, disappointments, and failures, then surely you're brave enough to take your sticks to the jungles of Central America.

At first blush, the countrysides of Panama and Costa Rica, El Salvador and Guatemala, may not strike the typical hacker, weaned on televised broadcasts of the PGA Tour's diagonally mowed fairways, as the ideal venue for chasing around a little white ball. But consider this: Latin America is warm, green, topographically varied, loosely populated, and perilously close to developing a full-blown case of Golf Fever, thanks in no small part to a young American fellow named Eldrick. Golf thrives in these lands of coffee and sugar cane, and with development plans in various stages of implementation, it's on the brink of becoming about one-one-hundredth as popular as soccer. As opposed to its current state of one-one-thousandth.

At present, there aren't many places to play golf in Central America. But there aren't many players, either. A busy day in Costa Rica might be 25 participants. Not 25 four-somes—which some muni courses in the States handle in about two hours—but something like two groups an hour.

Unless you happen to be a member at Las Vegas' ultra-exclusive Shadow Creek (*Raise your hand, Mr. Wynn!*), the only time you might see tee boxes so uncrowded in America would be in the middle of the night. And thanks to the vagaries of international currency exchange—let us take a moment to offer some silent praise to the global appeal of our humble dollar—green fees in this part of the world are a bargain. Okay, that's putting it delicately; compared to America, they're often *cheap*. Playing golf in Central America might give you some idea of how our Japanese friends must have felt on their annual pilgrimages to the resorts of Hawaii a few years back, in happier times for the yen.

❖ ❖ ❖

Unlike most of its Central American neighbors, Panama has a number of inexpensive, public, muni-style golf courses, including a few in Panama City, which, until recently, were largely used by members of the American military. Frankly, you're probably not going to want to play these decrepit goat tracks. Which is not to disparage the reputation of goat tracks. Their humble charms will do in a pinch. But you probably get your fill of them back home, and there's no sense in wasting a precious free day away from your business meeting (or whatever brings you to Central America) on unmemorable golf.

Instead, make a trip to Coronado, the Southampton of Panama, where the rich and powerful and their well-connected friends keep beach-side weekend homes. Getting there requires a 90-minute drive out of the city on the Pan-American Highway, passing through tiny villages packed with colorful food stands where fresh provisions of fruit and nuts are always at the ready. Your journey will eventually lead to the Coronado Club Golf Course, the chief amenity of the Coronado Hotel & Resort.

Designed in 1972 by George Fazio and his then-apprentice nephew, Tom (of the many top-100 credits), Coronado is the site of the Panama Open, a $30,000-first-prize event that attracts swarms of Nike Tour players trying to earn an exemption into the Sarazen World Open, a "silly-season" cash cow meant for, among others, national Open winners. Measuring close to 7,000 yards from the tips, Coronado is a true "championship" test, as opposed to the "championship" courses that real-estate developers suppose they create when building golf courses that are little more than electric-carts-required excuses for housing tracts. Coronado's design ethic is classical: The tees are proximate to the preceding green; the greens are sensibly free of gimmickry; and the layout traverses largely undisturbed land.

Several holes are what Americans might call "unfair," which is another way of saying "strategically challenging." The 13th, a 494-yard par-5, for instance, features a double fairway split by a grove of trees. On your second shot, you can choose to aim for either side of the trees or attempt a heroic carry over the trouble onto the green. Problem is, both sides of the fairway funnel directly into the trees, leaving anything that lands farther than 90 yards away from the putting surface in a timber prison. Your sole consolation, should you fall prey to this arboreal trap, is that this hole, as well as almost every other on Coronado, is home to several varieties (30, actually) of mango trees. Until you've taken a brief pause in your round of golf to pick yourself a juicy snack, you haven't really lived. (The 15th has a particularly fecund bunch near the green.)

When I visited in 1998, there were only two other groups on the course. This, I gathered, was slightly out of the ordinary—usually there are more like five or six groups. (And Coronado is generally recognized as the best course in Panama.) Conditions, I must report, were poor. Thanks to El Niño, whose wrath has been felt inversely in Latin America, leaving in its wake a wicked drought, Coronado was baked to a fine crust. Now, brown grass is fine; indeed, sometimes it's delightful. But a six-month absence of rain had left the place in miserable shape, especially the greens, whose exceedingly grainy turf could be heard crunching underfoot.

Now that a little water has come Coronado's way, a day here is a great deal. Hotel guests (many players choose to make an overnight trip of their visit) pay $25. On week-days, those who wish to return to Panama City after their golf may purchase a "facilities pass" for half ($65) the pre-vailing room rate (around $130), which includes day use of a room and all the facilities, including the golf course.

And all the mangos you can eat.

❖ ❖ ❖

Cariari Country Club, on the outskirts of San Jose, capi-tal of Costa Rica, is like the vintage Ferrari your uncle keeps under wraps in his garage: It's got the kind of classic beauty that makes you say silly things like, "They just don't build 'em like they used to" and "If it were mine, I'd drive it ev-ery day." See, Cariari is magnificent. But it's situated in the heart of a country that's home to something like 300 golf-ers. A place like this should have two-month waits for tee times; instead, it's basically walk up and play. I suggest you do your part when you're in Costa Rica and give this gem the kind of attention it deserves.

Like most of the better layouts in Latin America, Cariari was designed, in 1977, by the Fazios. In fact, this was one of George's last efforts and one of Tom's first. Built on a former coffee plantation boasting the kind of natural elevation changes and mature trees that any modern golf architect would kill for, Cariari is easily the most memorable golf course in Central America. It stretches to only 6,590 yards from the *azul* tees, but what it lacks in enervating length it compensates for with narrow fairways, lined on almost every hole by a nefarious strain of tree, known as the Ball-Gobbling Eucalyptus. Hit if off the short grass here and you can be sure to spend your round "feeding the monkeys," as the locals like to say.

Many holes require you to think your way through them, rather than merely rip a driver off the tee and flip a short-iron into the green. The 18th, for instance, is a par-4 of 382 yards. But you don't want to hit more than a 3-iron here, unless you want to "feed the fishes" in a creek that gurgles at the bottom of a steep slope, about 80 yards from the green. Similarly, the par-3 13th, 174 yards to a plateau green, seems upon initial consideration the kind of one-shotter that begs for a missile at the flag, which is usually placed on the left side of the putting surface. But anything left of the green—even two yards left—brings "feeding the lizards" into play, since there's a canyon that drops about 500 feet directly behind the pin placement.

One of the club's excellent caddies will alert you to your options, employing an effective mixture of deliberate Spanish and valiant English. Among the enduring charms of Cariari is that though you can rent an electric cart ($25), it's cheaper to take a caddie ($15 plus tip). Nearly everyone walks here and, unless you're suffering from some sort of physical infirmity, you've got to be crazy not to stroll the fairways. A prettier park setting you will seldom see.

To play Cariari, you must be the guest of a member— good luck in a country of 300 golfers! Alternatively, you can play if you stay at one of three nearby hotels: the Herradura, the Melia Cariari, and the Resedencia de Golf. The golf tariff is $40.

Should circumstances keep you from this splendid place, your best alternative is a new course in the suburb of Santa Ana, designed by an American, Tracy May, and called Valle Del Sol. There's hardly anybody ever there, so you can play three or four circuits ($30 day pass) without interruption. Green, curvaceous, and postcard-quality pretty, this is the kind of course that makes you think, "This *can't* be Central America."

❖ ❖ ❖

Of El Salvador's six million inhabitants, about 200 play golf. This is understandable when you consider that the annual per-capita wage in this ravishingly beautiful country is about $2,500, and the initiation fee at the nation's only

18-hole facility is $4,000. Given the economics, golf here has the pungent taint of elitism about it. The stark contrast between those who have and those who do not is no more evident than at the Club Campestre Cuscatlan, a splendid nine-hole course (with two sets of tees for an 18-hole match) set among dramatic hills in the heart of San Salvador, minutes from all the best hotels.

During the civil war that ravaged this country throughout the 1980s—"the trouble," as locals call it—guerrillas used to hide out in the woods adjacent to the fourth hole, occasionally letting loose a round of sniper fire. These days, El Salvador is a peaceful happy country. Still, beyond the fences that effectively separate the outside world from the finely landscaped prettiness of the golf course, people who will never be able to pay for a round of golf, let alone an oversized titanium driver, live in rotting shacks. And armed guards patrol the club's borders, keeping El Salvador's privileged few safe to hit their hooks and slices.

Fittingly, Club Campestre Cuscatlan does not welcome outside play. The only way to visit this well-designed, well-maintained, little layout is as a guest of a member. If you're doing business in San Salvador, chances are your local colleagues belong, or know someone who does. Also, some hotel concierges might be willing to "introduce" you to a member. Otherwise, you'll have to enjoy golf in El Salvador as the other 5,999,800 residents do: from the outside looking in.

❖ ❖ ❖

The Guatemala Country Club also employs armed guards. But this is not particularly unusual in Guatemala. Because of frequent kidnappings, many of the country's wealthy families hire bodyguards like Californians hire gardeners. Indeed, near the entrance to the country club, 10 minutes from the city center, there's a sign asking members to check their bodyguards at the gate and retrieve them after their rounds.

Happily, despite the heightened security, visitors are welcomed warmly. Guests of the Camino Real Hotel, in the Zona Viva, may play the Guatemala Country Club every day except Saturday and Monday for $50, plus a mandatory $15 caddie fee. And the club president tells me the Marriott, Radisson, and Princess hotels are putting together similar arrangements.

So you've never seen shotguns on a golf course? (Hey, unless you've been to Scotland, you've probably never seen a *dog* on a golf course.) I suppose this is one of the peculiarities of playing the game in this part of the world. But in every other sense, golf at the Guatemala Country Club is much like golf at an American country club, only better. The course, a muscular 6,630-yard layout framed by dense pine forests, is immaculately conditioned, with the finest greens in all of Central America. You often hear idle chatter about "not getting above the hole" on certain courses. This is the real deal. If you're not careful, downhill putts at Guatemala Country Club can easily roll off the green. Indeed, the whole course is fast, with firm close-cropped fairways that run forever. The fifth, a 642-yard par-5—no, that's not a misprint—seems, on the card, unreachable in regulation. But hit a couple of shots down the bowling-alley fairway and you've got a reasonable short-iron left to the green.

The 577-yard 15th, a classic risk-reward challenge, is one of the best holes in Central America. And the 211-yard 16th, an everything-in-your-bag par-3, is one of the prettiest. You'll likely take from your round here pleasant memories, and perhaps useful lessons. Because no matter your score, no matter the weather, no matter what business deal you did or didn't close on the 18th hole—none of that matters much. For playing golf in Guatemala, in Central America, is a rare and unlikely treat. And something it isn't back in America—a privilege.

27

GOLF
IN THE GULF

If not for the presence of men in white robes, women in veils, and traffic signs written in Arabic, a first-time visitor to Dubai, on the Persian Gulf, might imagine that his 16-hour, 12-time-zone, airline flight from America has somehow made a series of wrong turns and landed in Las Vegas.

Dubai, one of the best developed of the seven United Arab Emirates, is, like America's fastest growing city, an oasis in the sand, a booming metropolis, a business center, and a resort destination sprouting improbably from the desert. Everywhere you look, new buildings and roads and playgrounds are being built. Everywhere you look, money is being spent to make the place bigger and better and happier. And every day, they add more neon.

Once you check into your (state-of-the-art) hotel room, though, it doesn't take long to realize you're very far from home. Even the most exotic of Vegas suites do not have a helpful prayer sticker on the night table, pointing toward Mecca. Not even the most pampered of high rollers gets his five AM wake-up call performed outside his window by a chorus of wailing mullahs.

Unlike some of its scary neighbors across the Gulf, Dubai welcomes non-Islamic visitors with the kind of warmth and graciousness you might expect from the smiling hosts at Disney World. Up until the 1960s, before oil was discovered here, Dubai had been for centuries a community of seafaring merchants, who traded with the world from small wooden boats called *dhows*, which the curious traveler may still see floating on the wide creek that bisects the city. This is a polyglot culture, a nation of many colors, whose inhabitants are accustomed to dealing with strangers from strange lands. Moreover, they're generally a happy bunch. (Having one of the world's highest GDP per capita and almost no taxes, along with free education, free land, and free utilities, will do that for you.) This is not a country on the brink of a fundamentalist revolution. It's a country on the brink of a comprehensive—and costly—make-over.

Unlike, say, in Kuwait, Dubai's oil supply is finite. Palpably finite. Though government officials will not say exactly when this emirate will run dry, most people around the country assume the last barrels will be pumped in the next 10 or 20 years. Thus, Dubai has already begun transforming itself into a bustling trade zone, a magnet for corporate headquarters, and, bless their hearts, the premier destination in the Arab world for golf.

Bring on the tourists!

Though it may be a bit premature to call Dubai "The Classic Golf Destination," as the governmental PR brochures do, it's not too early to declare the country's finest golf course, Emirates Golf Club, one of the best facilities in the world. Indeed, in a poll conducted by the British publication *Golf Weekly*, of PGA European Tour pros, the Emirates Club ranked tops on the circuit, ahead of such stalwart competition as Valderrama, Wentworth, and Turnberry.

This is the golf course that hosts the increasingly infamous Dubai Desert Classic, the tournament whose six-figure appearance fees have lured most of the world's best players away from their home tours and into the Middle East. In past years, the Dubai event has been a lucrative part of the "silly season," the unofficial made-for-TV sojourn of winter golf, which most big-name players view as a low-pressure yearly annuity. The '96 edition of the Dubai

Desert Classic was especially irksome to tournament organizers in America where, because of a scheduling change,
Dubai's pay-for-play spectacle conflicted with the Bay Hill
Invitational, otherwise known as "Arnie's Tournament"—
Arnie being Arnold Palmer. If not for Palmer's personal
"discussions" with several American stars, including Corey
Pavin, many more would have defected to Dubai, where
the appearance-money fund is said to be substantially larger
than the entire tournament prize purse. Only Fred Couples,
the defending champion, opted for the easy cash.

Hosting world-class events like the planet's richest horse
race, international powerboating championships, and, naturally, the golf tournament gives the rest of the world a fa-
vorable impression of Dubai—and more impetus for tour
organizers to start booking golf vacation packages there.
Seeing Freddie and Greg and Seve playing on one of the
most immaculately conditioned courses outside of Augusta,
Georgia, affords the little emirate immediate legitimacy, if
not a huge audience.

So sparsely attended was the 1996 edition that when I
walked the final two rounds of the Desert Classic with the
leaders, I was afforded close-enough-to-see-their-pores gallery views of Ian Woosnam and Colin Montgomerie and,
yes, Mr. Couples that would be impossible in the States, or
anywhere else. A few roving groups of expatriates, carrying their national flags and following their countrymen,
roamed the course like a gang of happy fascists. But Saturday and Sunday are workdays in Dubai, and most of the
locals were back in the office, enjoying the rewards of toil-
ing in a country that imposes no personal income tax. I saw
a few golf lovers in robes and headdresses, but they generally confined themselves to the luxuriously appointed air-
conditioned skyboxes overlooking the 18th green.

The day after the tournament—won by Montgomerie—
I played the Emirates Club and can report that all the fuss
is certainly warranted. Though I shudder to ponder how
many million cubic tons of water, fertilizer, and chemical
compounds—not to mention dollars—must have been

dumped into the desert to construct this emerald carpet, the results are impressive. Emirates has, as you might imagine, plenty of sand bunkers to snare your errant shots, but there's a surprising amount of water and foliage, along with acres of good thick grass, too. (And flamingos.) The greens are among the hardest I've ever played. By that I don't mean "most difficult." I mean "most resembling a plateau of sun-baked asphalt." These are the kind of fast and firm putting surfaces that good players say they most cherish, but just try holding a 5-iron approach on them. Ironically, deep in the land of oil wells and camels, I found myself playing the kind of imaginative shots you'd expect to make in Scotland, land of bump-and-runs and sheep.

Though I'm seldom swayed by ancillary accouterments like locker rooms and snack shops—some of the world's best courses boast little more than shacks flanking the first tee—I was taken aback by the Emirates Golf Club's clubhouse, a sprawling glass-and-steel spectacle cleverly constructed in the shape of traditional Bedouin tents. It's a fine place to have a drink, tell stories about reaching the par-5 finisher in two, and imagine you're T.E. Lawrence with a 9-iron.

The clubhouse at Dubai Creek Golf and Yacht Club is even more stupendous. Opened in 1993, "the Creek," as the locals call it, has a long Karl Litten-designed course that's in many respects the equal of your typical American resort course—only about twenty times better maintained. Despite the magnificently intimidating finishing holes that run parallel to the banks of the eponymous creek, this serviceable course is overshadowed—literally—by the clubhouse, built in the shape of billowing sails. It looks like a cross between the Sydney Opera House and the Next Big Vegas Casino.

I played the Creek with a South African and a Canadian. The day before, my partners were Swedish and Finnish. During other rounds I was joined by Pakistanis, Brits, and Germans, in keeping with Dubai's international flavor. Nearly all the Europeans and Asians who play golf in Dubai at some point remark how unusual it is to be playing our beloved game in the desert. Whenever this happened, my first impulse was to tell them about this little place in southern Nevada ... but you get the idea.

To my taste, the most unusual location for a golf course in Dubai is not on what was once a vast expanse of sand. Rather, it's on the infield of a horse-racing track. The Dubai Golf and Racing Club, a nine-hole layout with alternate tee boxes to facilitate an 18-hole match, sits within a pitching wedge of the Nad al Shiba racetrack, where the American horse of the year, Cigar, won $2.4 million in the Dubai World Cup. (The course is closed during races.) Lacking even a single tree, the course has a decidedly "links" feel to it, with rolling mounds and pernicious pot bunkers, though you'll never mistake it for the Lancashire coast. Even more peculiar than its proximity to the ponies (all balls on the track are o.b.) is that the Dubai Golf and Race Club is completely floodlit, allowing for an experience you can enjoy at few facilities: night golf.

I'd played on lighted practice ranges before, but this was my first round under the halogen. Though my vision suffered from the contrast between dark air and luminous ground—okay, I couldn't see a damned thing—I enjoyed hacking it around in the coolness of the evening, with stars filling the sky. During the wicked summer months, I'm told, night tee times become nearly as precious a commodity as raw crude and potable water.

For the most peculiar (and one of the most enjoyable) golf experiences in Dubai, you need to visit the Dubai Country Club, an all-sand course (you carry around a patch of AstroTurf to hit off) with "browns" instead of greens. These delightful putting surfaces, built from hardened motor oil (!) topped with a fine mist of sand, give the truest roll of anything I've ever used the flat stick on. When you're done putting, you sweep away your footprints and the ball's demure little trail with a squeegee-like broom.

I've never seen anything like it. Not even in Las Vegas.

Thoughts for the 19th Hole

28

IN PRAISE
OF CADDIES

"The general conclusion ... is that the use of an electric cart is a problem for each country club. The survey suggests that only physically handicapped [players] be permitted to use carts."
—*Golf World Magazine; April 6, 1956*

Casey Martin and the Rules notwithstanding, golf, to my mind, is a game best enjoyed on foot. And if you don't agree, I suggest you board the next flight to Scotland and get back to me after you've walked a few rounds. Don't misunderstand, power carts—or buggies as they're known on the other side of the Atlantic—aren't evil incarnate. They're just antithetical to golf's greatest virtues.

Caddies, on the other hand, complement everything that's great about golf. Caddies are friends and teachers and psychologists; they are disciplinarians and confessors and helpers. And they carry the bag.

I love caddies. Whenever possible, I play with one. Regrettably, that's becoming increasingly difficult in these muddled days, when many golf resorts have not only eliminated caddies, but gallingly *require* players to use a cart, thus generating piles of rental revenue. (Hey, they need the cash; it takes a lot of money to build new golf

courses, especially ones with miles of asphalt cart paths.)
Caddies are under siege. If they're not being replaced by
motorized carts, they're suffering attacks from the IRS,
which had recently sought to classify caddies as employ-
ees of golf facilities, rather than as the classically independent contractors they are and always have been. Until several duffer-Congressmen got the IRS to change its way of
thinking, the few American clubs that still had caddie pro-
grams were thinking of doing away with their stable of
bag carriers altogether.

With the advent of high-profile caddies, like Tiger's
former looper, Mike "Fluff" Cowan, and Davis Love's
brother Mark, the average sports fan has become increasingly familiar with the caddie's role in a round of golf—
even if that sports fan has never employed one himself. With
added visibility, caddies are enjoying burgeoning appreciation, if not popularity. The USGA Museum recently put
together a traveling exhibition called "The Caddie Story—
Retracing the Steps," which documented the "evolution of
the eccentric and loyal" looper. And two of the best golf
books in recent memory, *A Wee Nip at the 19th Hole* and
Maybe It Should Have Been a 3-Iron, are about caddies at St.
Andrews and on the European PGA Tour, respectively. Still,
many players believe a caddie should merely "show up,
keep up, and shut up," for he is probably a drunk or a human mule or worse.

I've had caddies who relished a wee nip (whether they
were off the course or on) and caddies who were good for
little more than toting the sticks. But most of the caddies
I've played with have been knowledgeable, helpful, and
hugely entertaining. (You'll find good caddies everywhere,
but the best seem to reside in Scotland, where caddies are
still an integral part of the game.) Caddies have been responsible for some of my most cherished rounds of golf.

I'd like you to know a few of them. And not let them
disappear.

❖ ❖ ❖

After two decades of working at Turnberry, during which three Open Championships have graced the Ayrshire coast and fashions have come and gone, fickle as a putting stroke, Stevie, 51, has not adopted the modern visage of a PGA Tour caddie. Not for him are the neatly pressed slacks, crisp cap (with sponsor's logo emblazoned on the crown), and wrap-around sunglasses. He favors four layers of jumpers, chosen for utility, not color coordination. Extra towels are hidden beneath his clothes. His skin is worn like a fine old leather grip. With a briar pipe stuck between his craggy teeth, narrow eyes shrouded by giant eyebrows, and, it must be said, nostril hairs reaching halfway to his upper lip, Stevie looks every inch the Scottish caddie.

As he takes me round the links—"gettin' hoom," he calls it—Stevie regales me with tales of champions past, showing me the spot where Watson chipped in to draw even with Nicklaus in '77, where Price holed his 45-footer for eagle in '94, where Norman and Trevino and Daly hit this drive or that 1-iron. Or at least I think that's what Stevie was telling me. His accent, thick as the fog shrouding Ailsa Craig on a rainy day, is almost incomprehensible to American ears. But it's music, nonetheless. On the sixth, a par-3 called "Tappie Toorie" ("hit to the top"), Stevie hands me a driver and says, "'S too tweny-thrree ta tha muddle. An' gewd luck ta ya, sir!" On the 14th, a long par-4 called "Risk an' Hope," I ask where the name came from. "Yew'll fin oot, sir," he says, chortling. "Aye, ye will."

The day we play, the rain pours down in punishing sheets, drenching course, equipment, player, and caddie alike. The final three holes play directly into a 30-mph wind, which makes each raindrop feel like a stinging pellet. Wet, tired, and thinking of nothing more than "gettin' hoom," I hook my drive on the 17th into whin and gorse the height of a cow. Wordlessly, Stevie trudges off in search of my wayward shot. When we arrive in the general area, I quickly assess the hopelessness of the situation and tell him not to worry, we'll just play on and get this travesty over with. He frowns. "Sir," he says, shielding his eyes from the rain, "thar's na poin' a' loosin' a perfeckly good ball, sir." After five minutes of poking through the thorns, I almost have to drag wet Stevie away, reassuring him all the way down the 18th fairway that, in my eyes, his honor remains intact.

❖ ❖ ❖

Bruce, who has caddied for 31 of his 42 years, knows every inch of Western Gailes, a primal links not far from Glasgow—and does not suffer insubordination gladly. "That moond, oot beyon' tha gorse. *Tha's* yer line!"

He prides himself on almost never losing a ball, thanks to self-proclaimed eyes like a hawk. This seems hard to believe, since Bruce wears spectacles as thick as pint glasses. But after nine holes of expert ball sightings, green readings, and distance calculations, he reveals his secret. Alternately winking each eye, Bruce says, "Ah hae one eye fer shart an' one fer lang. Werks lacka charm."

❖ ❖ ❖

Some caddies are from the Don Rickles school of diplomacy. They leap at every opportunity to needle their players, to mock their weaknesses, and, by doing so, inspire their men to play better. Such antics walk a fine line between good-natured camaraderie and cheeky impertinence, and it takes a good judge of a stranger's character to know whether none-too-subtle teasing will be met with a grin or a stiff rebuke.

Niall, a veteran of Royal Troon, is such a caddie. After two duffed drives, which come to a sorry end 40 yards from the tee at the bottom of waist-high grass, he says to me, "Michael, I was under the impression ye had played this game before."

On the next hole, a par-5, he points to the sign beside the tee. "You see this, Michael? It says, 'Dunure; five-hunnert twenny-too yards; par-five.' Not par-fifteen."

When I shank a wedge approach from 110 yards, Niall

looks at me incredulously and says, "We have a word for someone who plays like this, Michael. And I'm afraid it's not 'golfer.'"

But when my game finally does come around and the pars start piling up like so many divots on a practice range, Niall is visibly pleased, an enthusiastic spectator who can barely contain his urge to cheer.

Caddies like Niall make every shot feel like it *matters*. Even when each shot is just a brief pause during your good long walk.

❖ ❖ ❖

Let us now praise Mr. Charlie Winton, 63, a resident of Perth, Scotland, who has worked at Gleneagles, in the nearby village of Auchterarder, for more than 25 years. Let us praise this good man and hold him up for adulation and admiration. Let us think of him and smile. For Charlie Winton is the best caddie in the world.

Where does one start? Perhaps with his kind face, smooth and untroubled, befitting a man 20 years younger. Perhaps with his soft lilting voice, which would never utter a cross word upon the links. Perhaps with his blue eyes, the color of the sky after a cleansing rain, which never miss a shot, no matter how wayward. Everything about the man instills comfort in his companions, despite the anxieties that sometimes infect a stroll from the practice putting green to the first tee. Charlie makes you feel that whatever happens on the golf course—shooting a new course record or taking a record number of shots—will be equally fine. And when you're walking the fairways with him, chatting about football or flowers, whisky or wind, everything about golf *is* fine.

This is not to suggest that Charlie Winton is indifferent to the shots you make. Oh, no. Charlie cares deeply about his man's round and provides comically precise lines of play, yardage distances, and ball-flight suggestions for nearly every shot, as though his man might actually be capable of reliably employing his advice. He adores golf's endless challenges, and he takes great pleasure in helping his client put together small pieces of a life-long puzzle. But even more, Charlie Winton wants his man to savor the fleeting thrills of splitting a fairway, hitting a green, holing a putt. He wants golf to be about little moments of joy.

That's why Charlie can be heard to utter words like "magnificent" and "magic" when you strike your ball well. That's why he will sometimes clap you on the back after a successful stroke and say, "Aye. *Tha's it!*" And that's why, when a well-struck putt, rolling along the path he has divined, finds the bottom of the cup, Charlie's lips curl into a restrained smile, his head bobs almost imperceptibly, and the slightest hint of jauntiness imbues his walk to the next tee. Charlie Winton's greatest joy on the golf course is helping his companion get it right in a game that so often goes all wrong.

Charlie has walked every yard of James Braid's courses at Gleneagles. He has seen places on the King's course you couldn't imagine exist and spots on the Queen's course you wouldn't want to visit even in your nightmares. He's carried for hackers who can't break 100 in nine holes and for touring professionals who play a game with which he is unfamiliar. He's seen movie stars and celebrity athletes, heads of state and titans of industry, good-natured old chaps and mean-spirited yobs. He's walked thousands of miles at their sides. And yet he never tires of his two-a-day circuits around these lovely paths in the park. There's always a new friend to be met, a triumph to be savored, a truth to be discovered.

There is always someone he can help.

Charlie Winton is a caddie. Men like Charlie Winton are what make golf great.

29

THE HEALER

When someone asks you, "What's your handicap?" you probably respond with a variety of numbers, depending on whether you are trying to impress someone or win a bet. "I'm a nine," you might say to a new business associate, or "On a good day? Fourteen," to your weekend $5 Nassau buddies. For most golfers, "handicap" is a measure of how much the game of golf has gotten the better of them.

For Gus Bernardoni, a PGA teaching professional from Deerfield, Illinois, "handicap" is an expression of how much in golf—and life—can be overcome.

In 1944, serving as a paratrooper with the 101st Airborne, Gus Bernardoni jumped out of a plane over Holland. His chute did not open properly, causing him to fall 300 feet onto a hostile bit of the Netherlands. Plummeting toward Earth, he had what he describes as "a talk with God," during which he asked Him to bless all the friends and loved ones he would never see again. Instantaneously, Bernardoni's body went as limp as wet newsprint. He lived and, understandably, became a lifelong Christian. But for 78 days on the front line, trapped under heavy fire, Bernardoni went without proper medical treatment, leaving his spine twisted and his right leg paralyzed.

After corrective spinal surgery restored movement to

the young paratrooper's lower body, doctors at the Mayo Clinic suggested that Gus swing golf clubs as part of his recuperative therapy. Employing all the tenets of a "correct" stroke—keep a stiff left arm and the head down, rotate the hips, and so forth—Bernardoni suffered excruciating pain.

But he didn't quit. He adapted.

"I found a way to hit the golf ball within my physical limits," Bernardoni explains, introducing himself to a small group of golfers at a Moline, Illinois, driving range. "You can, too," he says.

The golfers at this instructional clinic, sponsored by United Cerebral Palsy, are not looking to shave strokes off their scores. They're not trying to cure a troublesome slice. They don't want to play golf *better*—they just want to play golf.

And Gus Bernardoni wants to help them. "I *know* therapy can be difficult. I know the fear of working toward health and not being sure you'll ever get better," Gus says, pacing before the group, limping slightly. "But I also know there's somebody out there in worse shape than you. So you'd better start counting your blessings."

Telling someone like Mark De Vrieze, a paraplegic, or Don Smith, who lost the use of his left side to a stroke, to count their blessings might seem insensitive to some. Not Gus. "Let's not pretend we can do everything exactly like other people can. You may be 'less abled.' Maybe you can't walk or run too well. And maybe certain activities are hard for you. But you manage. So I don't want to hear about 'disabled,'" he tells the group of nascent golfers. "'Disabled' is someone who quits."

Gus informs his audience that he could have lain in a V.A. hospital and collected a pension, or convalesced at home. Or done nothing. Instead, he taught himself to play golf—not traditionally, but well. In 1974, still enduring chronic back pain 30 years after his parachuting mishap, Gus Bernardoni won the Illinois PGA Senior Championship. In 1978 he wrote a book, *Golf God's Way*, outlining his peculiarly effective methods. In 1993, he was inducted into the Illinois PGA Hall of Fame.

Bernardoni is a staff consultant to the Tommy Armour Golf Company, whose eponym, coincidentally, also overcame a host of physical ailments en route to golfing greatness. Now 74, Gus still plays out of the Pine Meadows Golf Club in Mundelein, Illinois, and coaches several Senior PGA Tour players, including the remarkable Joe Jiminez, who regularly shoots his age. But much of Bernardoni's life is devoted to work with the Special Olympics and hospitals around the country, coaching people with debilitating illnesses like multiple sclerosis, muscular dystrophy, and arthritis on how to develop self-esteem, confidence, and willpower through a game that normally inspires none of these qualities in its practitioners.

Today, on an autumn morning in the heartland, Gus Bernardoni is teaching this group of "less-abled" athletes that, despite their various infirmities, they, too, can hit a golf ball. "If you can do that, you can do just about anything. Just ask anyone with the use of all their arms and legs. They'll tell you the same thing," he jokes, flashing the kind of smile you tend to see on those who really like their work.

Gus tells his audience that golf is really a lot simpler than most people think. "You've got to get balanced, you have to swing the club, and you have to hit the ball. That's it," he says, shrugging. Most of the game is mental, he explains, so someone's coordination, or lack thereof, is hardly an impediment to making contact with the ball. "There's no such thing as 'mechanical positioning,' so no individual can copy anyone else successfully," Bernardoni says, growing impassioned. "Would you tell a blind man he 'looked up'? Would you tell a man with one leg he needs to 'shift and pivot' his weight on the backswing?"

To demonstrate, Gus hits golf balls from one foot, on his knees, and facing backward. And when I say "hits," I don't mean "makes contact with." I mean "*powders.*"

"You've only got one hand to work with? You can't see?

Can't use your legs?" Gus laughs. "You've got *this*," he says, pointing to his head.

Bernardoni calls up John Irwin, who, since a massive stroke, can move only his left side. Gus has Irwin tuck his right hand into a pocket. "Get that thing out of the way," he says. Then he adjusts Irwin's left-hand grip, turning all his knuckles on top of the club. Shifting Irwin's torso to the right of the target line to "redefine his center of gravity," Bernardoni asks his student to pick up the club and chop at the ball while exclaiming "Pow!" at impact.

"Pow," Irwin whispers, as the ball dribbles off the tee. Gus stands with his hands on hips, in mock disbelief.

"Not pow," Gus says weakly. "POW!"

His student laughs. But now he's all business. After a few emphatic practice swings, John Irwin addresses his ball, makes a mighty wallop, and yells "POW!"

The ball sails into the distance.

Everyone applauds heartily. But John Irwin doesn't notice. Holding his golf club out like a sword, he's too busy savoring every wondrous yard of the ball's flight, a journey that he, a massive stroke victim, engineered. When the ball finally comes to rest many glorious yards from where it started, Irwin shuffles, six inches per step, over to his chair. For the remainder of the morning, that golf club never leaves his hand.

The next time you're playing badly and want to throw a club or let loose a string of curses or behave with anything but dignified grace, imagine trying to play golf from a chair. Or with one arm. Or without sight. And then be profoundly thankful you have the limbs and faculties and ability to hit a golf ball, no matter how wretchedly.

Eric Black, 11, has spina bifida. From his chest down he has no sensation, and must be strapped into a chair. His pal Mark DeDecker, 12, has cerebral palsy and epilepsy, and is deaf in one ear. Like most young boys, these two love to watch sports on television, especially Mark, whose mom says he's nuts about golf. Mark dreams, as we all do, of one day making slam dunks like Vince Carter or hitting home runs like Ken Griffey Jr. or blasting drives like Phil Mickelson. But unlike other eager boys his age, Mark's dreams come true only in his imagination.

Mark DeDecker and Eric Black can only watch the Masters broadcast every year. They will never play golf at Augusta National. They will never know the thrill of making par on a championship golf course.

That's why, after a dozen earnest whiffs and much cajoling and coaching and encouragement from Gus Bernardoni, when Mark DeDecker makes a bold one-handed swing with his 9-iron and sends his ball airborne, flying free and clear from all his earthly despairs, I am not the only one watching who has a tear in his eye. With a shot of maybe 45 yards, Mark DeDecker has just eagled the Amen Corner of his dreams.

30

ALACRITY
AND DEMEANOR

A dear friend recently took up the game of golf, despite the warnings of many reasonable and caring acquaintances who told him he was surely headed up (and then down) a slippery Sisyphean slope. Golf, they told him, is the heroin of sports: It will alternately make you feel ecstacy and agony, and it's almost impossible to quit. "You are traveling on a road," my friend was counseled, "that never returns home."

Experienced players knew that my friend was voluntarily adopting a game that was difficult to learn, practically impossible to master, and just seductive enough that he would spend much of his remaining years in a comically futile pursuit of competence.

Better to take up tennis, they urged. Or knitting, perhaps. Less frustrating.

I did not concur—with the tennis part, that is. Yes, I told my friend, golf is frustrating and elusive and powerfully addictive. But that's not why we play the game.

We play golf for most of the usual reasons one plays any sport: competition and challenge and exercise. But we also play for less quantifiable purposes: introspection and serenity and boon companionship. We play for the magic.

Or should, anyway. The problem is, when your heart and mind and soul are not in perfect alignment, which is nearly always, it's easy to lose sight of what matters about playing golf. We become wrapped up in shooting a score, in striking the ball better than the week before, in hitting it farther and truer. In looking good. And inevitably we're disappointed. Yes, as Shivas Irons, the mystical Scottish hero of *Golf in the Kingdom*, says, there is no point in playing golf if you don't keep score, if you don't constantly measure yourself against yourself. But the point in keeping score, a true and honest score, is not to highlight one's imperfections; it's to highlight one's improvements.

Shortly before I commenced to play a round with my friend, I told him that he might want to keep score for himself, merely as a reference, a starting point from which to gauge his progress. But, I informed him, I would not be judging his golf game on the merits of his scorecard. His success or failure as a golfer, I told him, would be the product of two essential attributes, neither of which had any relation to being under or over par.

Alacrity and demeanor.

Alacrity and demeanor, I said. These are the hallmarks by which I measure the contents of a man's golfing character.

I don't care if you make quintuple-bogey on every hole. Play efficiently and pleasantly, I told my friend, and I will think you a terrific success at this silly and wonderful game. Play for the joy of being outside in a beautiful park with a companion who treasures your camaraderie. Relish the game's difficulties, rather than brood over them. Meet your small triumphs—a crisply struck iron, a drive that finds the fairway, a putt that rolls just where you wanted it to roll—with gleeful appreciation. Meet your predictable failures with graceful equanimity. Struggle with dignity. And do it without inconveniencing all the other strugglers waiting to play behind you.

Do all that, I told him, and I will consider you a magnificent golfer. And I will look forward to the pleasure of playing with you for many years to come.

My perspective on these matters, I confessed, came from

the experience of failure. Early on in my golfing career—if anything so consistently mediocre could be characterized with such a lofty phrase—I was a rotten player. And by rotten, I don't mean a bad scorer. (That goes without saying.) I mean I was a player who would interminably study a 10-foot putt from 14 different angles, all to win a grape soda from a childhood buddy. I would stand forever over iron shots, agonizing about "swing mechanics" for what must have seemed like hours to my patient comrades. I was a player who did not practice regularly, yet would throw his clubs in disgust when he played like someone who did not practice regularly. A player who would sulk over missed shots. Who would pout. And whine. In short, an altogether unpleasant miserable golfer who excused his bad behavior on the spurious grounds of "being competitive."

I'm older now, and a wee bit wiser. And though I occasionally have my shameful moments, I'm a far better golfer. My scores are a little better, too.

Happily, I have seen the correlation between a good demeanor and good scores in others. Jim, my regular playing partner in Los Angeles, was, when I met him, a club-throwing curse-muttering cloud of bitterness. Sure, he could hit the ball a mile, and when all the cylinders of his game were firing in concert, he could bring our local course to its knees. But when things went slightly awry—a missed putt, a heavy wedge—Jim turned ugly. He was no fun to play with, and he knew it. After several empty threats to quit the game, Jim had a therapeutic talk with his wife. From what I gathered, the discussion was chiefly about putting things in perspective and behaving like a grown man, about playing golf for enjoyment, not self-inflicted pain. Jim still hits the ball a mile, but now he manages his demeanor as well as his swing, and he has edited temper-related double-bogeys from his scorecard. The guy plays great *and* he's fun to play with.

In Scotland, where they know a thing or two about golf, slow play does not exist, because it's not tolerated. I have never played a round there, morning or afternoon, that took more than three and a half hours. And I've never felt rushed. Once, while I was searching for a wayward ball in the heather grass at Royal Dornoch, another group played right through, barreling past while I took two minutes or so to find my elusive orb. There was nothing acrimonious about this moment, no scowling glares or grumbled epithets, merely the tacit understanding that one either plays on or gives way.

Imagine such a scenario at your local muni course, where 25-handicappers take six practice swings, chunk their shots 40 yards, take two or three post-debacle practice swings, sulk disconsolately to their ball, and repeat the routine for an endless six hours. I don't begrudge people playing bad golf; we all start out (and sometimes finish) playing badly. It's no sin to take 8s and 9s on most holes; it is unforgivable, though, to do so slowly. Make whatever score you can, I counseled my friend, but do it with alacrity.

Slow play and quick tempers ruin a good round of golf more surely than a torrential thunderstorm. It's time, I suggested to my friend, that beginning players stop concerning themselves with swing plane and weight shift and reverse pivots. Kind instructors who really want to impart golf lessons that will last a lifetime should teach their students not how to strike their balls as well as, say, Tom Watson, but how to play with the man's noble spirit.

I choose Watson as an example of one to emulate—and there are many others—for the cheerful determination he has shown these past few years when his ball-striking has been as sublime as ever and his putting, especially from four to six feet, has been atrocious. While I don't care for some of Mr. Watson's off-course righteousness—he was instrumental in getting Gary McCord removed from the Masters telecast and infamously made unsubstantiated McCarthy-like allegations of widespread cheating on the PGA Tour—his on-course demeanor, while professional, is light-hearted and inspiring. Plagued by inscrutable problems with his putter, Watson has never once, as far as I know, thrown a club, shouted a curse, or growled icily at his caddie. He merely plays on. And when all does go well—as when he won the Memorial tournament at age 48—he allows a broad unguarded smile to brighten his boyish face, displaying for all the world a glimpse at the joy of getting it right.

On the other hand, we have the unspeakably talented Tiger Woods. Mr. Woods, it has been noted widely, is in many senses a role model, a ground-breaking stereotype-shattering trailblazer. He hits the ball far and shoots record scores and dominates major tournaments. He is a winner.

Tiger Woods, however, is not at present the kind of golfer we should be encouraging our children and friends to emulate.

First, he plays slowly. (He has already been fined and penalized for this.) Second, when all does not go exactly as he wishes, he pouts and whines and curses and mopes—even when he is leading the Masters or the U.S. Open by a jillion shots. Though he has made noticeable improvements—thanks, one suspects, to the adverse impact a nationally televised spew of expletives tends to have on an athlete's endorsement value—much of his demeanor is still that of an impetuous spoiled brat. Tiger Woods often behaves like a big baby who can't fathom the profound injustice of having his putt break nine inches when he read it for six. One hopes that with age, Tiger's tannins will soften. Indeed, Bobby Jones, whose legacy as a gentleman is unparalleled, began his storied career as a fiery and obnoxious time bomb, who early on walked off St. Andrews mid-round in a fit of pique. At the moment, though, Tiger Woods is not setting a good example. Should the new generation of players he is introducing to golf emulate not only his perfect swing but his frequently sour demeanor, the game will be worse off.

Tiger's apologists—among them the breathless announcers who know he boosts television ratings—attribute his sneering and head-shaking and frowning to being intensely competitive, to having an insatiable will to win. To being frighteningly focused.

Great. I applaud all that. But I think one of young Mr. Wood's many handlers ought to suggest to him that there are additional loftier targets on which he might try to focus. Like the ones my friend concentrated on during his inaugural nine.

My friend shot a bundle with me the day he took up the game. But he did so with alacrity.

He hit all manners of chunks, skulls, shanks, slices, hooks, and pop-ups. But he did so stoically.

He did not fret or rant or complain. He almost never commented on the quality of his play. He talked instead of the regal hawks flying overhead, the smell of the grass, the balm of the sunshine. He enjoyed the day.

And that's why I look forward to my next round of golf with this man. That's why I am proud to call him my friend.

THE END

Also by Michael Konik:

The Man With the $100,000 Breasts and Other Gambling Stories

ISBN 0-929712-72-2 • PRICE $24.95

A fearless gambler who got breast implants to win a $100,000 bet. A hard-core dice shooter who turned a borrowed stake of $10,000 into $17 million. A marketing genius who developed a "900" line for selecting winners of NFL football games—and had his 4-year-old son make the picks. These are some of the characters that populate Michael Konik's *The Man With the $100,000 Breasts and Other Gambling Stories*, a collection of the renowned gambling writer's best magazine pieces.

Konik, the long-time gambling columnist for *Cigar Aficionado*, ushers readers into the arena of risk and reward, introducing them to the subculture of high rollers, hustlers, professional card counters, horse handicappers, and poker champions. These stories take you to the final table of the World Series of Poker where a $1 million prize awaits the winner, to a secret golf course reserved for the biggest gamblers in Las Vegas, and to the inner sanctum of an international bookmaking operation.

Konik profiles America's greatest golf hustler and most accomplished blackjack cheat. He reveals the best and worst games in the casino. And he shares some of his own hilarious attempts at achieving gambling nirvana.

Entertaining and stylish, *The Man with the $100,000 Breasts and Other Gambling Stories* is a literary look inside the world of gambling.

About Huntington Press

Huntington Press is a specialty publisher of Las Vegas- and gambling-related books and periodicals. To receive a copy of the Huntington Press catalog, call 1-800-244-2224 or write to the address below.

Huntington Press
3687 South Procyon Avenue
Las Vegas, Nevada 89103
e-mail: books@huntingtonpress.com